Famous Barr

Famous Barr

ST. LOUIS SHOPPING AT ITS FINEST

EDNA CAMPOS GRAVENHORST

Published by The History Press
Charleston, SC 29403
www.historypress.net

First published 2014

Manufactured in the United States

ISBN 978.1.62619.692.6

Library of Congress Control Number: 2014953163

CONTENTS

DEDICATION

I believe in making your passion your purpose. My passion is telling stories through writing. In the retail industry, stories are told through public relations, special events and marketing. A savvy business storyteller brings in the crowds, and retailers need crowds to spend money in order to keep the doors open. Public relations, special events and marketing are all about telling a story that creates interest and generates sales to make a profit.

This portrait of Helen Weiss was taken in 1999. *Courtesy of the Weiss family.*

At Famous-Barr, it wasn't just about making the sale. It was also about entertaining customers to enhance their buying experiences. Many of these buying experiences are now memories that have a direct connection to Helen Weiss, the public relations and special events director at Famous-Barr for over forty-five years.

Dedication

I dedicate this book to Helen Weiss, the fiery woman known for her sense of style, bold jewelry and community service. Thank you, Helen, for keeping up with the public relations files throughout your years at Famous-Barr. Without these archives donated by Macy's Retail Holdings, Incorporated to the Missouri History Museum, this book would not be possible. We appreciate your years of service to Famous-Barr and the City of St. Louis.

Helen Weiss and Famous-Barr are no longer with us, but they continue to live today through our cherished memories.

FOREWORD

In the late 1950s and 1960s, Famous-Barr produced shopping bags emblazoned with the slogan, "You're Never Far From Famous-Barr."

That was so very true insofar as I was concerned. I found myself at Famous-Barr far more than I would have liked as an adolescent because my mother worked there. Her name was Helen Weiss, and she was in charge of public relations and special events.

Though I am pretty sure she didn't have to, my mother worked pretty much around the clock at her job. On many evenings, rather than hire a babysitter, she dragged me along to one of those never-far stores.

There she would spend hours schmoozing with managers, buyers and sales clerks while I entertained myself by wandering through the store, making funny faces in the mirrors in the costume room, thumbing through novels in the bookstore, eating samples at the candy counter and ordering up gelatin cubes with whipped cream in the Tea Room.

I had the run of the place until 9:30 p.m. when a recording of bugles sounded, signaling the store was closing for the night. I knew then I had yet another half hour to go because Mom just wouldn't leave until the security guards shooed her out.

I have to tell you that never being far from Famous-Barr was rather burdensome for me. But for my mom, it was anything but. She loved those stores and everything in them, especially the people. Had I been paying more attention, I would have appreciated that Mom wasn't just having fun nor just working a job. She was making history along with thousands of others who made Famous-Barr into a special place where St. Louisans didn't just buy stuff. They made memories. Just about everyone of a certain age in St. Louis can recall a special moment at one of the Famous stores, whether it was the first time they laid eyes on Santa, tried on a confirmation or prom dress or met a movie star.

That's why I am so grateful that Edna Gravenhorst has produced this wonderful book that describes a golden age in St. Louis retailing. My mom worked at Famous-Barr beginning in 1962 and would not retire until 2007, when she was eighty-one years old. That was long after the May Department Stores Company sold the Famous-Barr stores and all of its other properties around the nation to Macy's. It took a lot of persuasion to get Mom to retire. She was afraid she might die once she left. And, in fact, one year later, she did.

Gone, too, are the legends who made Famous-Barr so great: Morton "Buster" May and Stanley Goodman—perhaps the best known—but also Joan Van de Erve, the hard-driving marketing executive; Jerry Loeb, a former May Department Stores Company chairman; and Eula Fulton, the legendary buyer in women's fashions.

Of course, Famous-Barr was a great place even before my mother got there, as Edna recounts. Mom just wanted to be part of it all. How she got there is a bit of a story in itself. Like many women of the '50s, Mom did not have her sights set on a career. She played mah-jongg. She did volunteer work. When she wasn't campaigning for Democratic candidates, she was working for the Nursery Foundation, which had an annual event called the Book Fair. It was held in the Clayton Famous-Barr parking lot. That's how Mom got to know the people at Famous and talked her way into a part-time job coordinating special events.

They didn't pay her much. I remember the store manager—as a joke—gave Mom her pay in a candy box filled with shiny coins where the candy would go. Had he just given her the Mavrakos chocolates, she likely would have come out ahead. And, of course, those bean counters at the May Department Stores Company knew that my mom would spend her earnings and more at Famous on earrings, shoes and the latest designer clothing. That's how she rolled. She always looked great. (That's a gift she passed along to my sister, Jean, also a fashion plate and also a backer of worthy social causes.)

The May Department Stores Company got its money's worth—and more—from Mom. Helen Weiss was a prime mover behind Famous-Barr, sponsoring the first Independence Day celebrations under the Gateway Arch, the forerunner of Fair Saint Louis. She introduced St. Louis women to the Wonder Bra by having it roll up in its own limousine. She hosted such stars and luminaries as Sophia Loren and Elizabeth Taylor, Mickey Mantle and Ozzie Smith, Julia Child and Craig Claiborne. And she was a tireless advocate for worthy causes and initiatives, including making the stores more accessible to the disabled and advocating for the store to have both black and white Santas.

Of course, she was not above some flim-flammery. There was the time when Famous-Barr was promoting merchandise from Spain and planned an event featuring Spanish flamenco dancers. At the last minute, the dancers called to say they couldn't make it. Mom got in touch with some folks of Hispanic origin on St. Louis' south side. They put her in touch with some dancers. The troupe arrived just in time—from New Mexico. To maintain the illusion, she instructed them not to talk with anyone in English.

Other than that, I'd have to say my mom was an exemplary role model. You don't have to take my word for it. There are legions of women who worked with my mother who say she blazed a trail. One of them is the legendary Maxine Clark, who worked for the May Department Stores Company before going on to be the founder of the iconic Build-a-Bear Workshop. "She taught me not to fear people in power—particularly men," Maxine said at Mom's funeral service. "No one was too important or too unimportant to Helen—she had a heart and soul enough for all of St. Louis."

My mother gave her heart and soul to Famous-Barr and always considered it a bargain. Thanks to Edna for honoring her and all the people who made Famous-Barr a heavenly place.

RICHARD H. WEISS
Author, Editor, Writing Coach
Weiss Write, LLC
St. Louis, Missouri
June 2014

ACKNOWLEDGEMENTS

Writing and researching a book is a team effort. The time involved affects family and friends, and if you are lucky, they understand your commitment in telling the story that needs to be told.

First, I would like to say thank you to my husband, Ted Gravenhorst. His patience and support got me through the months required to write this book. Next, I would like to say thank you to all my family and friends who waited patiently through short visits and short phone conversations to allow me the time I needed to focus on this project.

A big thank you goes to my friend and fellow colleague Jim Merkel for recommending me to editor Ben Gibson at The History Press. Ben, I appreciate your patience and support throughout the book process. You were always there on a timely basis with the information I needed.

I would like to express my gratitude to my friends and acquaintances who supported me by giving me information, references and encouragement: Joan Briccetti, Linda and Charlie Dalheimer, Cheryl Fillion, Bill Hart, Esley Hamilton, Scott Tjaden, Cathy Frank Sherman, Yolanda Reed and Fred Zeller with the City of St. Louis.

I am grateful to all the professional and expert staff members at the Missouri History Museum Library & Research Center, especially Molly Kodner and Dennis Northcott, archives; Jaime Bourassa and Amanda Claunch, photographs and prints collections; Gwen Moore, curator of Urban Landscape and Community; Randy Blumquist, librarian.

Acknowledgements

The most enjoyable part of the research for this book was my visits with Ethel Foster, Manfred P. Zettl, Susan Fadem, Richard H. Weiss, Diane Rademacher, Sandy LaRouche, Shirley Barken, Sam Clark, Frank Scheithauer, Becke Sneed and Marcel Toussaint. I appreciate the time you took to find photographs and visit with me so I could tell a more complete story of Famous-Barr.

INTRODUCTION

NINETY-FIVE YEARS OF SHOPPING, CELEBRATIONS AND CREATING MEMORIES

In 1911, the May Department Stores Company acquired the William Barr Dry Goods Company and combined it with its Famous Shoe and Clothing Company and established Famous-Barr. This would be the beginning of St. Louis shopping at its finest and set the stage for a retail business that would last almost a century.

When I write books, I am asked, "Is your book a complete history?" The story is not always that simple, and a book can only tell part of the story. Every chapter is a small sample of what was going on at a certain time. It is a limited recording of the past to encourage readers to bring forth their own memories of their times at Famous-Barr. We all have our own memories, our own stories and narratives that give us a sense of place.

I hope that in reading this short version of the Famous-Barr story, readers will be inspired to share their own histories at Famous-Barr through photographs from family collections. Please post them on the Famous-Barr Facebook group page. This will add to the legend of a store where there was so much more than shopping; it was a place where lives took place. For customers and former employees, it was a place where we shopped, worked, celebrated and created memories. It was a backdrop where we established our sense of fashion and style as we went through the different phases in our lives.

As with any good tale, the story of Famous-Barr gives us hope and reminds us that our great country was built by immigrants who came to the United States in search of better lives. William Barr and David May were both immigrants who came to America in their teens, worked hard and obtained the American dream of prosperity. Their success improved the lives of St. Louisans for generations.

The May Department Stores Company had the foresight for a retail business that formed the foundation that would carry Famous-Barr through ninety-five years of enhancing the shopping experience. This basis for business attracted some of the most creative people in visual merchandising, display and public relations. Helen Weiss and the rest of the Famous-Barr associates understood the May vision and took pleasure in creating events to delight their customers. Bringing in celebrities and staging elaborate sales promotions brought in crowds of shoppers; a few were there just to look, but most of them were there to buy. The idea was to bring foot traffic into the store to give the salespeople the opportunity to sell. Famous-Barr wanted you to spend money and enjoy spending it. This was apparent during the holiday season. Christmas brought in big dollars, which generated profits. In turn, these profits helped fund the community events Famous-Barr sponsored.

The success of Famous-Barr was apparent when the company expanded to Clayton. Then it added stores in St. Louis County and built stores in other cities in Missouri and across the Mississippi River in Illinois. While Famous-Barr was spreading out, the May Department Stores Company was acquiring more retail outlets. By 2003, May Department Stores Company was operating 445 department stores in forty-five states, including the District of Columbia and Puerto Rico.

In 2006, the May Department Stores Company, which had been acquiring other companies for decades, was bought out by Macy's Incorporated. It was a sad day in St. Louis when the Famous-Barr signs came down and were replaced with Macy's. A chapter in St. Louis history came to an end, and we were left with our memories.

Chapter 1

FROM IMMIGRANT TO MERCHANT PRINCE

William Barr

William Barr & Company [has] *the distinction of being the greatest retail dry goods house west of the Mississippi.*
—Pictorial Saint Louis

William Barr was born in Scotland on October 7, 1827, in a little village named Lanark, in Lanarkshire. In 1840, at the age of thirteen, he immigrated to New York. The following year, he began his training in dry goods by going to work for Ubsdell, Pierson & Company. Barr's destiny and foundation for his life career began with this first job, which paid him a salary of two dollars a week.

Barr worked hard, and his employers rewarded him by giving the young man more responsibilities. In 1854, Ubsdell, Pierson & Company sent Barr to take charge of a branch house it had established in 1849 in St. Louis. Mr. Joseph Franklin, the manager of the New York branch, accompanied Barr on his first trip west.

The St. Louis branch house had been opened under the name H.D. Cunningham & Company as a business branch of Ubsdell, Pierson & Company of New York. The branch was managed by Mr. Cunningham and operated under the Cunningham name until 1854, when the partnership expired. The expiration of the partnership offered William Barr and James Duncan the opportunity to join the partners of Ubsdell, Pierson & Company as partners in the St. Louis operation. In 1860, the partners of the company were listed in the St. Louis city directory as J.A. Ubsdell, Charles Pierson,

This portrait of William Barr was taken in 1900. *Courtesy of Missouri History Museum.*

William Barr, James Duncan and James J. Cubbage. The business offered dry goods at retail and wholesale at Fourth Northeast Street at the corner of Vine. At this time, William Barr resided in St. Louis on Carr between Fifteenth and Sixteenth Streets.

The company continued doing business as Ubsdell, Pierson & Company until 1863. In 1864, the company name was changed to Ubsdell, Barr, Duncan & Company. Then, in 1867, it became Barr, Duncan & Company. The partners were James Duncan, Joseph Franklin and William Barr. By 1870, William Barr had become the senior partner in the St. Louis store, and the name was changed to William Barr & Company. The partnership consisted of William Barr, Joseph Franklin and Charles H. Bering. While the store was going through partnership and name changes, the business continued to grow. With this growth came the need for larger locations. The store had started out at the corners of Third and Market Streets, later moving to the corner of Fourth and Olive Streets. By 1875, William Barr & Company, the retail dry goods store, included notions, ladies' shoes and millinery goods. The store covered an entire narrow city block between St. Charles and Vine Streets, extending from Fourth to Third Streets.

The William Barr & Company store building was four stories high, and according to a business biography in *Pictorial Saint Louis*, published in 1875, Barr's was "a spot where feminine feet love to tread." There were over three hundred employees on the payroll, consisting of salesmen, porters, cash boys and the staff members in the working, packing and delivery rooms. The thirty-two departments ran as shops within the store, responsible for keeping their own books and earning profits for the company as a whole.

The Third Street front of William Barr & Company Dry Goods House is visible in this 1876 image. *Courtesy of Missouri History Museum.*

The manager of each department was held accountable for its inventory and once a month reported sales and merchandise on hand to meet their sales volume. Daily orders were sent to the New York office to replenish the merchandise sold. The buying was done by business partner Charles H. Bering, who lived in New York. Joseph Franklin, one of the other partners, managed the store in St. Louis. William Barr divided his time between his home and offices in the east and St. Louis.

In 1855, Barr married Jessie, the daughter of John Wright, in New York. The couple had no children, and they resided in Orange, New Jersey. Their residence was located in Llewellyn Park, at a mansion named Baronold.

Women loved to shop at Barr's, a place where they could buy both their dry goods and fashionable apparel. The first floor housed dry goods consisting of flannels, linens, domestics, ribbons, hosiery, notions, gloves, embroideries and laces. Also on the first floor were dress goods, silks, gentlemen's furnishing goods and fabrics. On the second floor were suit and cloak rooms with departments for shoes, hosiery, underwear, upholstery goods, quilts and hats. The general business offices where the bookkeeping was done were located on the third floor, along with workrooms for the hats, quilts and upholstery goods departments. The third floor was also where most of the store printing was done in its own printing office. Workrooms for the suit and cloak departments were on the fourth floor. An area of the basement was used as a stockroom and service area for wrapping goods that would be delivered to customers. The rest of the basement served as the salesroom for toys. Shoppers could go from floor to floor and to the basement with ease because the store had installed safe hydraulic elevators.

William Barr had spent years establishing himself as a merchant, and in 1875, the company bearing his name was considered to be the third-largest dry goods retailer in the country. It was time to diversify his business holdings. He decided to invest in real estate. A block west of Lafayette Park, in one of the best neighborhoods in the city, Barr decided to build a block of red brick houses, a total of seven dwellings. The location was in proximity to the center of the city where his business interest was located, and it was close to the courthouse. The townhouses were offered to lease at $700 a year, equaling $58.33 per month. The tenants who resided at 2618–2630 Lafayette Avenue, or "Barr's Block," were businessmen who were well known in St. Louis society circles.

The William Barr Dry Goods Company continued to grow. In 1880, it moved to a building occupying an entire block on Sixth Street, covering an acre of land. Barr understood the importance of female shoppers. He hired salesladies to sell them the latest fashions in clothing and home furnishings. If alterations were necessary, the shoppers worked with a custom seamstress and had their purchases delivered to their homes when they were completed. The ladies could meet their friends in the Tea Room to discuss the latest fashion trends and gather ideas for their wardrobes from the clothes displayed throughout the store. These displays made shopping easier and more fun.

This is the north side of Olive Street, between Sixth and Seventh Streets in downtown St. Louis in 1882. *Courtesy of Missouri History Museum.*

The attention given to female shoppers created more jobs for women in the department store.

The details for the shopping experience could be seen throughout the interior and exterior of the remodeled building. Ladies arrived for their shopping excursions in carriages, making a second entrance necessary. An entrance was added on Third Street, in case the parking spaces were full at the entrance on Fourth Street. The ladies were also given special attention when planning the second-floor balcony, which looked down to the first floor. The balcony area was planned as a locale where ladies could gather and meet their friends for some local gossip and exchange of the latest news in St. Louis.

The female aspects continued on to the third floor, where there was an elegant suite with drawing rooms where the ladies could try on clothes and be fitted by attentive salesladies. The store claimed, "There is no retail establishment West of New York that equals that of William Barr & Company."

The William Barr Dry Goods Company occupied the blocks bounded by Sixth, Olive and Locust Streets in 1909. *Courtesy of Missouri History Museum.*

William Barr was already going to go down in St. Louis history as a successful merchant, but he secured his legend in the city even more in February 1877. He purchased a tract of land on which the Barr Branch Library would be constructed in 1905–06. Right after Barr bought the property, he sold the parcel to the Mount Calvary Building Association. The association had grown from the Calvary Protestant Episcopal Church, which had been organized in 1870. In 1871, well-known philanthropist Henry Shaw had donated a lot at Lafayette and Grand so the church could build its house of worship. The church was built, and the congregation grew so fast that in a few years, it needed a larger building.

In March 1877, the Mount Calvary Building Association was organized for the purpose of acquiring a new lot for the construction of a new larger church. The association found the parcel of land needed; the property belonged to Mr. Barr. The property was acquired, and construction began in September 1877. The church was a one-story brick building at the corner of Jefferson and Lafayette Avenues. The architect hired was Theodore Link, who later became a well-known St. Louis architect, but in 1877, this was his first project in the city. One of his greatest accomplishments was designing and supervising the construction of Union Station in 1893–94.

In a few years, the Mount Calvary congregation outgrew the building Link designed, so in 1885, a one-story addition was added. With the new addition, the church functioned well until 1896. When the Great St. Louis Cyclone ripped through the city, leaving a pathway of destruction behind, one of the casualties was Mount Calvary Church. The church building was completely demolished. It is assumed that the church did not have insurance on the building, and the property went into foreclosure in 1897. On the day of the foreclosure sale, William Barr purchased the property and once again became the owner of the parcel at Jefferson and Lafayette Avenues.

In 1903, William Barr donated the property to the board of directors of the Public Library of St. Louis, following the example of Andrew Carnegie. In 1901, Carnegie had gifted the St. Louis Library Board $1 million. There were three conditions attached to the gift. First, $500,000 had to be used for a central building, and the other $500,000 was to be used for branch libraries. Second, the city had to secure the sites for the buildings. Third, an appropriation of $150,000 annually had to be maintained for the library system.

In 1905, the Barr Branch Library was designed by Theodore Link. It was built for $72,000 in 1905–06. The official dedication was held on September 17, 1906. The library, located at 1701 Jefferson Avenue, is still serving the needs of the community.

Before the turn of the nineteenth century, even though there was competition on the retail side from Scruggs, Vandervoort & Barney Dry Goods Company and other smaller companies on Fourth Street, business continued to improve for William Barr Dry Goods Company at Sixth from Olive to Locust. By 1885, Barr's also had competition on the wholesale side of the business from Rice, Stix & Company on Broadway at the southeast corner of St. Charles Street.

According to the 1890 city directory, William Barr and Joseph Franklin were running the wholesale and retail business. Mr. Franklin resided in St. Louis, and Mr. Barr traveled back and forth from his residence in Orange, New Jersey. The company continued to grow, containing thirty-one departments by 1896. The business was still dealing in retail and wholesale. Dry goods businesses in St. Louis were doing well—not just Barr's but also its wholesale competitor. Rice, Stix & Company moved from Broadway to larger quarters on Washington Avenue at the southwest corner of Tenth Street.

The beginning of the twentieth century still found Barr and Franklin running the business. Their advertising boasted, "Missouri's Greatest Store Barr's, St. Louis at Sixth, Olive and Locust streets, one whole block." Their city directory listing read, "Quality Always the Best, Prices Always the Lowest. Everything in the way of Dry, Fancy and Staple Goods manufactured on the two hemispheres can be found at Barr's its quality is such that they can guarantee it. Save time, money and fatigue by doing your shopping at Barr's."

William Barr continued as president of the company until 1905. In 1906, his wife's brother, George M. Wright, became president. Mr. Wright continued on as president through 1909, with George H. Allen as vice-president and general manager. In 1908, Thomas H. McKittrick was added to the company as a vice-president. Now the company had two vice-presidents, Mr. McKittrick and Mr. Allen. McKittrick was also president of Hargadine-McKittrick Dry Goods Company at 911–19 Washington. It can't be said for certain, but it is safe to assume that with the death of William Barr in June 1908 and the business having grown to fifty-one departments of wholesale and retail, it was necessary to add a second vice-president with the experience of running a dry goods company.

William Barr died on June 16, 1908, at his home in New Jersey. The store in St. Louis was closed on June 18, the day of his funeral. His will was dated May 13, 1908, and probated in New York. At the time of his death, Mr. Barr and his wife resided in Llewellyn Park, West Orange, New Jersey. The article in the *St. Louis Globe-Democrat* read, "Mr. Barr's benefactions to St. Louis charities are the largest since those of the late R.M. Scruggs, who died a few years ago." Barr left $100,000 to Washington University, making it the largest sum ever willed to the university. There had been larger gifts by wealthy citizens of St. Louis, but they had been direct gifts and not bequests by will. The money was to be used through the William and Jessie Barr fund in the Manual Training Department. The Barrs were supporters of Washington University, believing it was the institution that could provide the best college education in St. Louis. Five to six years prior to Mr. Barr's death, the Barrs had given an estimated $30,000 to the university's general fund.

St. Luke's Hospital and St. Louis Children's Hospital each were given $10,000, while the Episcopal Orphans' Home, Protestant Orphans' Home, St. Mary's Infirmary, Bethesda Memorial Home, Home for the Friendless and the Blind Girls' Home each got $5,000. Mr. Barr also left $5,000 each to the Orange Memorial Hospital, Orange Orphan Society and the Record Ambulance. Other sums totaling an estimated $150,000 were left to relatives.

The two executors of his will each got $50,000, leaving Mrs. Barr with an estate worth $4 million.

In 1910, Thomas H. McKittrick stepped up to run the company as president, while George H. Allen continued as vice-president and general manager. In 1911, the William Barr Dry Goods Company was sold to the May Department Stores Company for $1,750,000.

Mrs. William Barr (Jessie Wright) died in January 1917 in Llewellyn Park, Orange, New Jersey. Following in her husband's footsteps Mrs. Barr willed $100,000 to Washington University, but this time it was to provide fellowships and scholarships for girls. St. Luke's Hospital, St. Louis Children's Hospital and Martha Parsons Free Hospital for Children and the YWCA received $25,000 each.

Through the continued use of the Barr Branch Public Library for over a century, the Barr family name has been etched in St. Louis history.

CHAPTER 2

FAMOUS AND MAY COMPANIES

JESSE W. MOTTE, JOSEPH SPECHT AND DAVID MAY

Mr. David May, of the Famous and Barr Dry Goods Company, is a living epitome of the department store idea.
—"St. Louis To-Day," the Mirror, *May 9, 1912*

The business of Famous-Barr was around for almost a century, yet few people questioned the "Famous" part of the name. Barr was obvious, and the history of the William Barr Dry Goods Company is well documented, but the challenge was in finding the early history of the Famous Clothing Company. However, the Famous-Barr story could not be told without the knowledge of the origin of the "Famous" in Famous-Barr.

In 1874, Jesse W. Motte owned a store that sold boots and shoes at 714 Franklin, and Joseph Specht was the supervisor at the store, known as Motte's. The following year, Mr. Specht was promoted to manager. In 1876, Motte and Specht became business partners and added clothing to the store's inventory. By this time, the business was located at 703–705 Franklin and known as Famous Clothing Company. In the city directory, it was listed as Famous, Motte & Specht. It sold civil and army clothing, boots, shoes and related merchandise.

The Famous history continued in an article printed on May 15, 1876, in the *St. Louis Post-Dispatch.* The title read, "Famous," with the subtitle, "Famous for What; For Being the Cheapest Place in St. Louis." According to the article, Motte and Specht had opened a small store on Franklin Street around 1870 with very little money. To attract customers and build their business, they

The Famous-Barr Department Store occupied the lower floors of the Railroad Exchange Building, which covered an entire city block consisting of Olive, Locust, Sixth and Seventh Streets. This image is from the early 1900s. *Courtesy of Missouri History Museum.*

sold their goods for small profits. Soon they gained the reputation of the place to go if you were looking for a good deal. People would remark, "No. 714 is the famous place for bargains." In 1876, customers still referred to the store as No. 714 (714 Franklin) even though the store had moved across the street. Motte and Specht overheard the "Famous" remark so often that they decided to incorporate it into the store's name. The partners knew selling quality merchandise at low prices was good for business.

The new larger building across the street from the old store provided them with the space to display their goods in better fashion. The chandeliers, which were lighted at night, helped with advertising, and each globe was marked "Famous." At the entrance of the store, there was a sign on each side with a painting of a man pointing down to the words, "This Place is Famous."

In the 1880s, the Famous Dry Goods and Clothing Company was at Broadway and Morgan. In an advertisement in the *Veiled Prophet's 6th Annual*

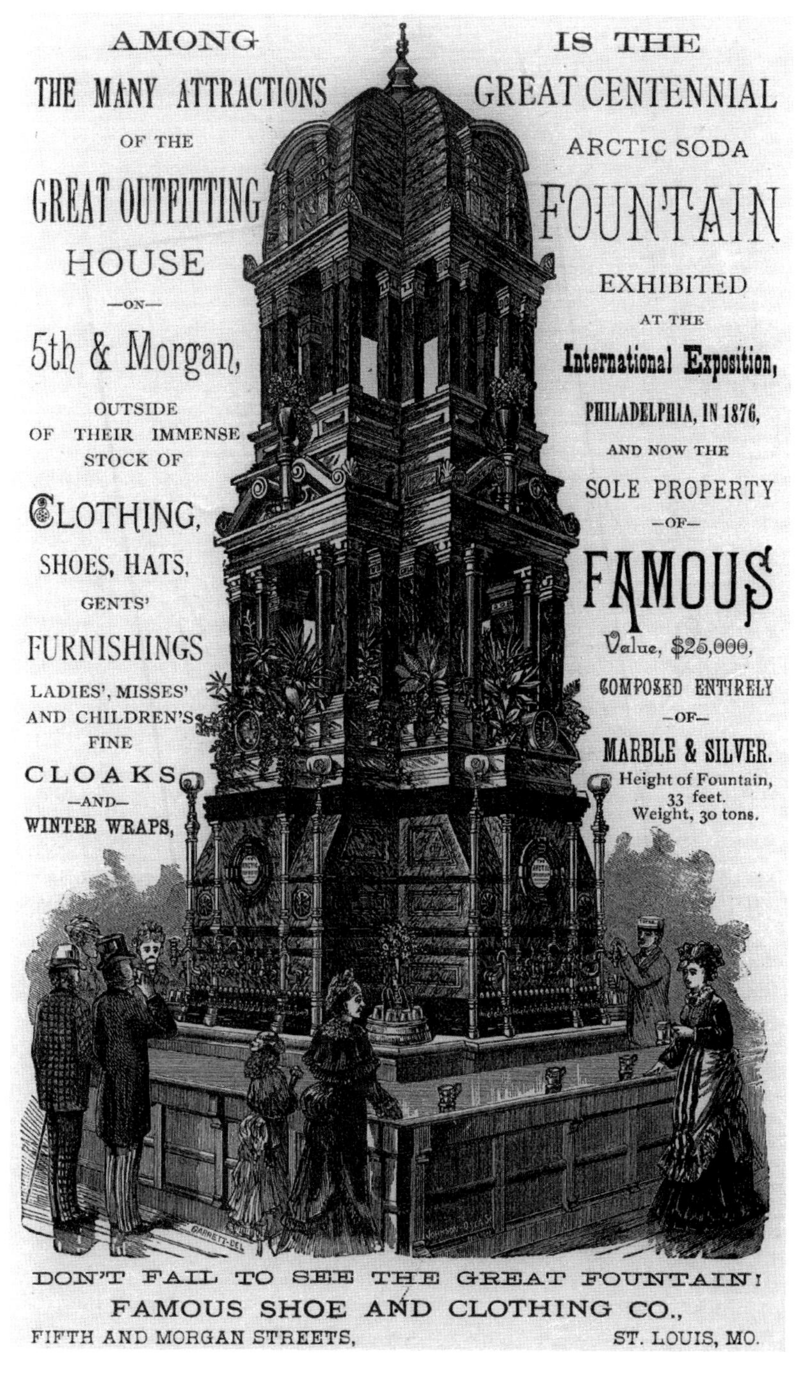

This image was an advertisement in 1883 for the Famous Shoe and Clothing Company featuring its Great Centennial Arctic Soda Fountain. *Courtesy of Missouri History Museum.*

Autumn Festival Magazine dated October 2, 1883, the "Great Centennial Arctic Soda Fountain" at Famous was featured. The soda fountain mixed fruit syrups with soda water for "refreshing drinks." It was a sign of how successful the business had become; the fountain cost $25,000, a very large sum at that time.

In 1892, with Joseph Specht as president of the Famous Shoe & Clothing Company at 514 Washington, the company was sold. David May and the Shoenberg brothers of Colorado bought the store for $150,000 in cash.

Joseph Specht died in Virginia, and his body was brought back to St. Louis for burial. His obituary in the *St. Louis Post-Dispatch* dated September 16, 1902, read, "Remains of the Former Millionaire Merchant Arrived, at Union Station This Morning Accompanied by Members of the Family." According to the article, Mr. Specht was born in 1851 in St. Louis. When he lived in St. Louis, he resided on West Pine. At the time of his death, his ninety-year-old mother was still a resident of St. Louis and lived on Russell Avenue. His former business partner Jesse W. Motte died in 1903. Motte's obituary read, "One of the founders of the Famous Department Store, longtime business associate of the late Joseph Specht."

David May was born on June 3, 1848, in Kaiserslautern, Germany. Like William Barr, he was also an immigrant. He left Germany for New York in 1863, at the age of fourteen. Soon after his arrival in New York City, he left for Cincinnati, where he had an uncle, and went to work in a clothing factory, making five dollars a week. May worked by day and studied English by night at a local college. He didn't want to stay at his factory job too long and soon went in search of a better job. He found one as a salesman, selling lithographs of the 1868 presidential candidates door to door to the citizens of Cincinnati and also to stores. He was good at sales, but being a peddler was just one step up from being a factory worker. May had ambitions and, to his good fortune, met a Mr. Kirschbaum, who owned a clothing store in Hartford City, Indiana. Kirschbaum was so impressed with the young man's selling skills that he offered him a job in his store.

May accepted the sales job and made his move to Indiana. He was paid twenty-five dollars a week, plus room, board and washing. The hours were long. Some days he worked from 6:00 a.m. to 11:00 p.m. He worked hard for two years, and as a result of his dedication to his employment, annual sales increased from $20,000 to $100,000. It was time for David to ask for a share in the business. He did just that and was rewarded with a one-quarter interest in the store. Now the sign over the store read, "Kirschbaum and May."

May remained at Kirschbaum's until 1877, the year that a fire broke out in the store during winter. May went in and out of the cold, trying to save as much of the inventory as possible. As a result, he came down with bronchitis, which developed into asthma, leaving his lungs weak and susceptible to tuberculosis. He sold his share in the business for $25,000 and headed to the dry, sunny climate of Colorado. There he teamed up with Jacob Holcombe and tried mining for a while, but it was grueling work with little success.

The failure of a merchant in Leadville led to an opportunity for the failed miners. May and Holcombe bought the inventory and the canvas shack it was housed in and set up shop. Thomas Dean, a local merchant, joined them as a third partner, and by September, the business was up and running. They named their store Holcombe, May & Dean Dry Goods and Clothing Merchants. It was May who started buying large quantities of riveted work pants favored by the miners in the area. These riveted pants later became known as Levi's jeans. Their business continued to grow as they added more inventory, including red woolen long underwear, which they sold for the under-the-market price of one dollar. This was the start of what would become the May Company Empire.

David May had a natural ability of knowing what products his customers wanted, and those were the items he stocked in his store. While May saw business opportunities, his partners were conservative. The business in Leadville was booming, and real estate prices were going up, so May decided it was time to build a permanent store. Holcombe and Dean were not in agreement, and the partnership was dissolved on good terms.

Dean opened up his own business, and Holcombe stayed on to work with May, later working for the company as an accountant and bookkeeper. Holcombe was still employed by the May Department Stores Company when he died in 1925. May's new store opened up on New Year's Day in 1878 as the Great Western Auction House and Clothing Company.

In 1879, David May met his future brother-in-law, Moses Shoenberg. The two young businessmen had plenty in common, as the Shoenbergs were well-known merchants in Leadville. This led to May and Shoenberg opening up a store on January 3, 1880, that sold clothing, boots and shoes. By August 1880, David May and Rosa Shoenberg were married. They made their home in Leadville, where they were part of the town's social circle and soon started their family. Morton J. May was born on July 13, 1881, and then came Tom on June 3, 1883; both were born in Leadville. Wilbur followed on December 28, 1898, and Florence May on February 27, 1903; both were born in Denver after David May sold his business in Leadville and bought a bankrupt store in Denver in 1888. In 1889, Mr. May moved the family to Denver. Morton J., Tom and Wilbur would grow up to become executives in the May Department Stores Company.

Soon after 1880, the Leadville headquarters were expanded. The business was growing, and May & Shoenberg began opening store branches in other mining towns in Colorado. The new stores were short-lived, however, and Shoenberg was ready for a change. In August 1885, he sold his share of the Leadville business to May and moved his family east.

The business climate in Leadville had been declining, and by early 1889, the economic situation had gotten worse. While Leadville was in decline, Denver was growing, as the railroads had turned a mining town into a city. It was time for May to leave Leadville. He had been preparing and had sold his business to Meyers Harris in late 1888 and bought a business from a bankrupt merchant in Denver for his new start. In January 1889, the May family moved to Denver.

Soon Mrs. May's brothers, Joseph and Louis Shoenberg, joined May in Denver to help with the business operations. They operated the business in temporary quarters for a few years, and in 1900, they moved the business to a permanent location downtown. The new store, May Shoe and Clothing Company, was located at 1614–20 Larimer Street.

In 1892, David May and the Shoenberg brothers purchased the Famous Department Store in St. Louis for $150,000. They continued to buy other department stores in other cities, and in 1905, the May and Shoenberg families made the move to St. Louis, which would later become the May Department Stores Company headquarters. The Mays and Shoenbergs adjusted well to their new home and took an active part in St. Louis social circles and the community, donating generously to local charities.

The May Company had been operating two stores in St. Louis, Famous and the May Company Store. The May Company Store operated from 1904 to 1908. On February 15, 1908, the May Company building at the northeast corner of Sixth Street and Washington Avenue became the new home of the Famous Department Store, which had outgrown its building at Broadway and Morgan Street.

In 1910, the May Department Stores Company was incorporated in New York. The following year, May Department Stores Company added to its empire by purchasing another St. Louis business, the William Barr Dry Goods Company. The purchase price was $1.75 million. May combined the two St. Louis companies into the Famous-Barr Company. Also in 1911, the May Department Stores Company had begun its listing on the New York

Left: This is a portrait of David May. The year it was taken is unknown. *Courtesy of Missouri History Museum.*

Below: The May Company Store at the southwest corner of Franklin Avenue and Broadway is seen in this photograph from 1906. *Courtesy of Missouri History Museum.*

Stock Exchange. That year, Morton J. May was listed as the director, with his business address at 519 Washington and his residence at 18 Washington Terrace. Both the May Department Stores Company and the Famous Shoe & Clothing Company were listed at 519 Washington.

David May died on July 22, 1927, and his son Morton J. May took over as head of the May Department Stores Company. Morton worked at May Company for sixty-seven years, he retired in 1967. After his retirement, the grandson of David May, Morton D. "Buster" May, took over as the chairman of the company until 1972 when he retired. According to an article published in the July 28–August 3, 1986 issue of the *St. Louis Business Journal*, "Buster May was the last descendent of David May to head the May Department Stores Company."

Chapter 3

LET'S DO LUNCH

Famous-Barr Restaurants, Chefs and Cooking Demonstrations

Never let them leave hungry.
—Helen Weiss in conversation with Sandy LaRouche, 1978

As early as 1914, Famous-Barr had a restaurant called the Dairy Lunch Room. Some of the items listed in the 1915 menu are not the items you'll find at most restaurants today. For five cents, you could eat a tongue sandwich, ten cents would buy you a sardine sandwich or you could order a sandwich made from meats we are familiar with today: ham, roast beef, chicken or corn beef hash. There were also dairy dishes, such as a bowl of milk with crackers or bread for ten cents. A steak dinner with French-fried potatoes cost a little more at twenty-five cents. You could also order German-fried potatoes for five cents. Desserts and pastries were a special treat, and you could order baked apples, custards, puddings, chocolate éclairs, pies, ice cream, stewed prunes, Charlotte Russe and ice cream, apple dumplings or half of a grapefruit. The prices for desserts ranged from five to fifteen cents. There was also a good selection of beverages priced from five to ten cents, including malted milk, malted milk with egg, coffee, tea, instant postum, milk, grape juice, buttermilk, milk and cream or sweet cider.

For the next few years, the menu at the Dairy Lunch Room had very few changes, but the one change that stood out in 1918 was that it no longer offered German-fried potatoes. Instead, they were simply listed as fried potatoes. This was indicative of the times. With the United States and Germany being enemies during World War I, German Americans did not want to be viewed as traitors in the United States. They stopped speaking German, and many of the German-language newspapers shut down.

America was at war, and changes had to be made to support the war effort. In 1918, Famous-Barr Tea Room signed an agreement with the Women's Central Committee on Food Conservation in cooperation with the United States Food Administration Committee for St. Louis. The agreement was to observe meatless Tuesdays, no-wheat Wednesdays and no-pork Saturdays until the food administration declared it was no longer necessary to observe the agreement. Famous-Barr restaurant employees were asked to help out with the war conservation efforts to consume less wheat, meat, fats and sugars in order to help supply food to American troops abroad.

The Tea Room, which was on the sixth floor and open from 9:00 a.m. to 5:30 p.m., was a great venue to celebrate special occasions and holidays. In 1915, for thirty-five cents the ladies could have lunch and be entertained. The store started entertaining their women customers during lunch with its Luncheon and Fashion Revue. If the ladies were in a hurry, they could have the Shopper's Salad Luncheon, which was also offered at thirty-five cents. If they had children with them, the youngsters were treated to Children's Day in the Tea Room for twenty-five cents.

From 1915 to 1920, afternoon tea was offered in the Tea Room. For fifteen to twenty cents, a customer could choose from an assortment of sandwiches, have ice cream for dessert and drink coffee or tea. In 1928, the afternoon tea was replaced by the Matinee Luncheon, which was served from 2:30 to 5:00 p.m. and cost forty cents.

Shoppers who did not have the time to eat lunch or take an afternoon tea break had other choices. The Dairy Lunch Room in the basement had a full menu of "wholesome, appetizing foods served promptly at popular prices." Another choice was on the Main Floor: the Magnificent Soda Fountain, which served sandwiches and soft drinks. If customers wanted to take candy, bread, pies or cakes home with them, the store had the Candy Shop and its own bakery.

Customers were not the only ones having lunch at Famous-Barr. For a small fee, employees could eat in the employee cafeterias. Before the Civil Rights Act of 1968, the employee cafeterias were segregated. Blacks had their cafeteria on one floor, and the cafeteria for whites was located on a different floor.

As seen in the photograph on page 38, the African American ladies were good looking, well groomed and sharp dressers. According to Ethel Foster, who was hired in 1947 as an elevator operator, you also had to be a light-skinned black to work at Famous-Barr.

Some Distinctive Features about this Foremost St. Louis Store

WAITING, READING AND WRITING ROOMS—*Third Floor*

Spacious and with pleasant, restful furnishings, this will be found an ideal place to meet friends or pass leisure time down town.

CIRCULATING LIBRARY—*Seventh Floor*

Thousands of volumes give practical assurance of your getting the books you wish to read, at the nominal charge of one cent a day.

CANDY SHOP—*Main Floor*

Large assortments of delicious Candies that were made in our own shop. Try our $1.00 Par-Excellent Line.

MAGNIFICENT SODA FOUNTAIN—*Main Floor*

Large, conveniently located and serves Soft Drinks, Frozen Dainties and Sandwiches.

DAIRY LUNCH ROOM—*Basement*

Wholesome, appetizing foods served promptly at popular prices. Full menu.

BAKERY—*Basement Salesroom*

Which bakes the lightest bread, pies, cakes and other delicious pastries, from the best condiments and sells them at popular prices.

BEAUTY PARLOR—*Main Floor Gallery*

Satisfactory service with skilled operators in attendance for manicuring, shampooing, hairdressing, massaging, etc.

CHILDREN'S HOBBY-HORSE BARBER SHOP—*Main Floor Gallery*

Where children enjoy having their hair cut.

POST OFFICE SUBSTATION—*Main Floor Gallery*

Stamps sold, Money Orders issued, Mail registered and Parcels insured. Mail collected here at regular intervals throughout the day.

EMERGENCY HOSPITAL—*Eighth Floor*

Fully equipped and experienced nurse in attendance.

BUREAU OF PUBLIC SERVICE—*Main Floor Gallery*

Luggage may be checked here and other service received without charge.

GAS AND ELECTRIC BILLS MAY BE PAID ON Main Floor Gallery

PLAY ROOM—*Sixth Floor*

A delightful place for children to play while mother does her shopping. Equipped with merry-go-round and many other amusement features. Experienced nurse in attendance.

MUSIC SALON—*Sixth Floor*

Hear the Ampico in the Chickering Piano—the masterpiece of musical instruments which reproduces the playing of the great artists with absolute fidelity. Superb facilities for choosing a Victor, Cheney or Brunswick Phonograph and new Victor or Brunswick Records.

MLLE. MODISTE MILLINERY SALON—*Fourth Floor*

A show place of unusual beauty and interest, where smart millinery creations from the leading fashion centers appear in wide variety.

COSTUME SALON AND MISSES' STYLE SHOP—*Fourth Floor*

The spaciousness and artistic furnishings of these Shops provide a handsome setting for the most authentic apparel from foremost designers.

SPORTING GOODS GOLF AND AUTO ACCESSORY SECTION—*Sixth Floor*

Complete lines and painstaking service insure satisfaction.

MEN'S CLOTHING SECTION—*Second Floor*

The largest men's clothing floor in America.

This is the back cover of the 1920 menu for the Tea Room at Famous-Barr explaining the store's customer features. *Courtesy of Missouri History Museum.*

This photo of the employee Christmas party in the black employee cafeteria at Famous-Barr was taken in the late 1940s. *Courtesy of Missouri History Museum.*

Ethel has fond memories of walking down the street with her work girlfriends and being called "Famous girls." Famous girls had good hair, were beautiful and had nice figures. It was something to be proud of to work at Famous-Barr. Mrs. Foster tells us, "You had to be first class because you were representing the company."

Their elevator-operator training consisted of how to walk and proper body image and emphasized appropriate conversations on the elevators with customers and among themselves. Mrs. Foster tells us that they were told, "Don't talk about personal stuff." She goes on to tell us, "Famous-Barr lady employees were classy, and they looked the part." Of course, looking the part meant they had to maintain themselves, because blacks were not allowed in the ninth-floor beauty salon where other women could have their hair done and their nails manicured.

On October 6, 2002, Greg Freeman wrote an article titled "Activist Pursued Fairness and Justice" in the *St. Louis Post-Dispatch*. He states: "In 1947, blatant racial inequality here was commonplace. Blacks were restricted in where they could live, where they could go to school, where they could work, even where they could eat." He goes on to talk about the sit-ins of

The chefs in this picture are Chefs Watzlawek, Manfred, Dan and Ned in the Famous-Barr downtown kitchen. They were photographed in 1966. *Courtesy of Manfred P. Zettl.*

1960 and how long before then the Dagens and the St. Louis branch of the Congress of Racial Equality (CORE) were already boycotting the lunch counters downtown. He mentions, "They also boycotted Famous-Barr and the old Stix, Baer & Fuller stores here."

As changes were taking place in the country, there were also changes at Famous-Barr. The company was expanding and opening up more stores, and more stores meant more restaurants. It was time for Famous-Barr to bring in an executive chef with European influence. Eric Dahl, the food service director at Famous-Barr, hired Manfred P. Zettl.

Chef Zettl came to the United States and arrived in New York in 1963, when he was twenty-three years old. His friends and sponsors in the United States were members of the Painter family from the Midwest Rubber Reclaiming Company in the St. Louis area. Zettl came to St. Louis and then left for a brief time to work at the 1964 World's Fair in New York. When he returned in the fall of 1964, he was hired for the position of executive chef for all the Famous-Barr restaurants and employee cafeterias. He is best known for perfecting the onion soup recipe at Famous-Barr that people are still raving about today. During his time as executive chef, he hired a staff of nine French bakers at the downtown location to make the baguettes for the company, while he and his staff did the cooking for the St. Louis Room. This dining room was the main restaurant at the downtown store and could seat up to four hundred customers. With more sophisticated dining, there was a need for a full bar. Famous-Barr had a liquor license and served alcoholic beverages in the St. Louis Room and the Tea Room.

The Famous-Barr French onion soup was such a hit that the stores opened up a soup substation named Soup Con. The Soup Con was located on the second floor in every Famous-Barr store.

Zettl worked at Famous-Barr for ten years, leaving the company in the fall of 1974. Manfred P. Zettl is a member of the American Culinary Federation Chefs de Cuisine Association of St. Louis. In 1987, he was the recipient of the Chef of the Year award.

There were many luncheons to raise money for charities at the Famous-Barr restaurants downtown. When the Clayton store opened its restaurant, the Wedgewood Room, it also became the scene of many fundraisers. One of the most elaborate fundraisers was the Around the World luncheons in 1961. The fundraiser was a series of six luncheons to benefit the Experiment in International Living, a nonprofit educational organization that was founded to create a better understanding of the world and its people.

Sitting on the committee for the Around the World luncheons were Mrs. Pierce W. Powers, Mrs. Richard B. Dempsey and Mrs. Ancel Whitsett. The Mexican luncheon, "Colorful Mexico," and the French luncheon, "Bridges of Paris," were directed and produced by Marcel Toussaint. The guests at the Mexican luncheon were serenaded by singer Maria Elena Chavez and guitarist Alfonso Santa Cruz from the Los Hermanitos Santa Cruz band. On stage, Marcel Toussaint and his younger sister, Odette Comer, performed the bullfighters dance, *pasodoble*.

In the late 1960s and 1970s, there was no Food Network and very few cooking shows on PBS. Famous-Barr, along with other department stores, saw the opportunity for cooking demonstrations in their housewares departments. At Famous-Barr, the cooking demonstrations and food shows took place in the Market Place. Just like fashion shows, these cooking demos generated sales. Two of the most recognized names—even if you are not a foodie—who appeared at Famous-Barr stores are Julia Child and Jacques Pépin.

Famous-Barr also featured local St. Louis chefs, including its own executive chef Jan G. Verdonkschot. Besides cooking demonstrations, Chef

Marcel Toussaint and Odette Comer dance the *pasodoble* at Clayton Famous-Barr in 1961. *Courtesy of Marcel Toussaint.*

Verdonkschot also taught cooking classes for kids. The class was called Petits Chefs. Each summer, kids from ages eight through fifteen could enroll for morning or afternoon classes in a three-day cooking program. Classes were held in the ninth-floor auditorium at the downtown store. The classes were limited to forty-eight children, with a fee of twenty-one dollars per student. Besides learning how to cook, students learned food prep and how to use sharp knives correctly. Chef Verdonkschot did a great job with the kids. Brandon and Laurel Johnson, the children of Sandy LaRouche, who worked in public relations at Famous-Barr, took part in these classes and are good cooks today.

Chef Verdonkschot was born in the Netherlands and started his culinary career at the age of fourteen during World War II. After the war, he went to pastry school and held several culinary positions before coming to St. Louis and landing a job at the Chase Park Plaza. He also worked as a chef for the Missouri Pacific Railroad and as the executive chef at the Missouri Athletic Club. From there, he went on to become director of hotel and food operations for Grove Manufacturing. Verdonkschot then spent thirteen years as executive chef and food service director for May Department Stores

Company, retiring after thirteen years of service. Verdonkschot is a member of the American Culinary Federation Chefs de Cuisine Association of St. Louis. In 1966, he was the Chef of the Year Award recipient and in 2007 was the Dubois T.C. Chen Award recipient. In 2010, Verdonkschot was the Oliver H. Sommer Mentor Award recipient.

David Guempel was among the other St. Louis chefs who did cooking demonstrations at Famous-Barr stores. Guempel, a self-taught chef, started his career at Duff's in 1976 and went on to Balaban's. Additional chefs at Famous-Barr included Atiba Nickens, who owned the Sunshine Inn on Euclid; Malvi Doshi and David Landau, who took part in the Beautiful American event; and Ellen Cusumano of Kemoll's Restaurant, serving Sicilian dishes in St. Louis since 1927. Chef David Slay, chef/owner of La Vernada Restaurant at 201 South Twentieth Street, prepared Bananas Foster for customers in 1990. La Vernada was known for its modern Italian cuisine, and the restaurant started operating in the lower level of the Drury Inn Union Station in 1988. Chef Slay's demo was to help promote the Stearns & Foster (mattress company) sale. He appeared at the Famous-Barr stores in South County, Northwest and West County in the Mattress Department.

While Famous-Barr brought in national celebrity chefs, it also supported local chefs, including Simone Andeyar, executive chef of the Grill; Andy Ayers, owner and chef at Riddles Penultimate Café and Wine Bar; Michael Jones, chef at Redel's DeBaliviere Place; William McGough, chef at Broadway Oyster Bar; and Richard Perry, chef at Richard Perry Restaurant.

Julie Dannenbaum opened her first cooking school in 1964 in Philadelphia. She would have a cooking school in that city for twenty years. She went on to write five cookbooks, writing her last one in 1984, but before that, she was at Famous-Barr. In 1968, she came to demonstrate her cooking skills to the citizens of St. Louis. To everyone's delight, Dannenbaum demonstrated basic skills for beginners and also trained cooks who had more experience.

In 1976, world-renowned French chef Julia Child came to Famous-Barr in St. Louis, where she demonstrated her informal approach to French cuisine in the Clayton store's third-floor auditorium. The following year, French chef Jacques Pépin came to St. Louis with Craig Claiborne, the restaurant critic for the *New York Times*.

Pépin and Claiborne were in the city to take part in "Food Fair" at Famous-Barr. In Jacques Pépin's autobiography, *The Apprentice: My Life in the Kitchen*, published in 2003, Jacques talks about the time he and Craig Claiborne were in St. Louis. They were in the city to raise money for a charity, and their main focus was to conduct cooking demonstrations. But Claiborne, who was

In this photograph, Chef Jacques Pépin is doing a cooking demonstration at the Famous-Barr Food Fair in 1977. *Courtesy of Missouri History Museum.*

always looking for new restaurants to introduce to his audience, wanted to visit as many St. Louis restaurants as possible. Pépin got to the point where he thought they had already experienced every eatery in St. Louis, but Claiborne wanted to try one more, a Chinese restaurant. Claiborne was a trained French chef who believed Chinese cuisine was the equal of French cooking; he didn't want to leave the city without trying a Chinese restaurant. They just happened to be in St. Louis when the Cardinals were playing in the World Series. An officer from the mayor's office was sent to their hotel with tickets to a home game, along with an invitation from the mayor to join him and a few others in his box at the stadium. Pépin laughs, "Craig immediately declined, stating we had to go to a Chinese restaurant." The gentlemen would have been better off watching the ballgame with the mayor. Imagine two New Yorkers looking for the ultimate dining experience in St. Louis at a Chinese restaurant. Pépin recalls, "A Chinese restaurant? And a lousy one, as it turned out."

Employees are making fudge in the Famous-Barr candy kitchen in 1979. *Courtesy of Missouri History Museum.*

The candy kitchen was located at the St. Charles Street warehouse down the street from Famous-Barr. There was an underground tunnel from the warehouse to the store, making the transporting of goods much easier. The kitchen made candy and fudge for all the Famous-Barr Candy Counters. However, not all the candy offered at the stores was made by Famous-Barr.

In October 1983, the "Famous New Carmel Apple" was introduced at Famous-Barr. It was made daily in the candy kitchen. A Jonathan apple was hand-dipped in a special caramel, and then it was rolled in fancy large pecan pieces. The apples were then distributed to the Famous-Barr stores.

The Famous-Barr restaurants and cooking demonstrations played a key role in the grand-opening festivities of new stores. When the Chesterfield store opened on August 3, 1983, the St. Louis Grille was packed with diners. Famous-Barr executives Ken Wilkerson and Richard L. Battram were also in the midst of the crowd. Battram had become the Famous-Barr president in 1976, and Mr. Wilkerson went on to become chairman of Famous-Barr in 1985.

In 1985, Vince Bommarito and two of his three sons, Vince Jr. and Anthony, took part in the remodeled downtown store opening in St. Louis Centre. They prepared culinary samples at the Famous-Barr cooking island

The Chesterfield Famous-Barr grand opening crowd is pictured in the Saint Louis Grille in 1983. Standing are Ken Wilkerson and Richard L. Battram. *Courtesy of Missouri History Museum.*

on the seventh floor. This was the floor that housed cookware and was named the Market Place.

Sandy LaRouche has many fond memories of her experiences at Famous-Barr involving the culinary arts. Sandy worked in public relations with Helen Weiss from 1978 to 1989. She was employed as the special events coordinator and the assistant public relations director. Helen and Sandy's event plans usually involved food. They had to supply the food for special events and the cooking demonstrations. It was also Sandy's job to make sure the celebrities and their staff members were fed before or after making personal appearances, which took some planning to coordinate with the celebrities and security. Sandy chuckles as she reminisces about the lengths she went through to make sure the celebrities had enough to eat. Then her expression saddens as she says, "Helen always told me, 'Never let them leave hungry.'"

Chapter 4

CHRISTMAS AT FAMOUS-BARR

Toyland, Santaland, Bearland

Stores wish you a Beary Christmas.
—Famous-Barr advertising in the St. Louis Post-Dispatch,
November 29, 1986

The ninth-floor auditorium and the train windows at Seventh and Locust Streets at the Downtown Famous-Barr was where most of the Christmas magic took place. The downtown store opened its animated Christmas widows on Thanksgiving Eve. It was the highlight of the week in St. Louis and the beginning of the holiday season.

On December 14, 1985, Helen Weiss was interviewed by the *St. Louis Post-Dispatch.* The article, "Miracles Are Worked Here Year Round," was hilarious and gives us an insight into Helen, who would go to great lengths for a successful and entertaining promotion, especially at Christmas. One holiday season, she got a cow up to the ninth-floor auditorium at Downtown Famous-Barr. She related to the interviewer, "One night when a fire alarm was accidentally triggered, the panicked cow broke out of its stall and was found in the luggage department." Another Christmas she worried about who was going to take care of and feed the three little bears that spent Christmas at Famous-Barr after making appearances in the Christmas windows. One Christmas she had a small zoo at the downtown store, consisting of a partridge, two turtle doves, three French hens and four calling birds for the twelve days of Christmas. Helen actually had them in the store for "twelve days plus a month."

The exterior six-story Christmas tree at Seventh and Locust Streets at Downtown Famous-Barr was photographed in 1960 and featured on Christmas store gift boxes in the 1960s. *Courtesy of Missouri History Museum.*

In 1963, Famous-Barr advertised, "Opening Tomorrow! Famous-Barr's 5 Santa-hosted Toylands." Each store—Downtown, Clayton, Southtown, Northland and South County—had its own Toyland. The Downtown store was open from 9:00 a.m. to 5:30 p.m., while the other stores were open from 9:30 a.m. to 9:30 p.m. The same advertising listed the Downtown store holiday attractions, including "the seven-story Christmas tree at 7th and Locust Streets; the animated window scene from Dickens's *Christmas Carol*, the series of windows reminiscent of Christmas 'past,' peopled by Christmas 'present;' the fabulous trains and freeway window and the bright red carpeted aisles on the first floor." In all of the five stores, children could meet and confide in Santa Claus in person. While they visited Toyland, parents and kids could take a look at "the Merry-making toys, games and giftwares." In the Downtown store, Santa greeted the holiday guests in the Downtown Exhibition Hall on the ninth floor, where there was an animated scene from *The Night Before Christmas*. Children were encouraged to visit Santa in his Victorian house, while the parents were reminded not to forget the prize packages offered at $0.39 for the youngsters. These packages were only available at the downtown store. Free comic books were given out to children ten years of age and under. Pictures with Santa were offered at $1.50 each or three for $3.50. In the downtown store, the entire eighth floor was devoted to toys, and Famous-Barr boasted of having the largest toy department in St. Louis.

While the children were intrigued by Toyland, the ladies were tempted to pick up gifts for themselves. Famous-Barr advertised "Little Furs at non-luxurious little prices." Four-skin natural Emba Autumn Haze mink sets or three-tier natural Norwegian blue fox capes were $125, brown-dyed squirrel cape stoles or three-skin natural stone marten sets were $100 and black-dyed Persian lamb jackets with natural mink trim were $299. For women who couldn't afford furs, there were Famous-Barr Basement Economy Stores. Each branch store had a basement economy store. The Pre-Holiday Sale at the basement stores advertised savings for the entire family.

According to the *St. Louis Globe-Democrat*, the newspaper that printed the photograph on page 50 on November 25, 1960, Christmas shoppers were lured downtown by their 136-page Thanksgiving Day *St. Louis Globe-Democrat* edition. The day after Thanksgiving, people flocked downtown to see what was new and start their holiday shopping. Christmas display windows at the Downtown Famous-Barr were a destination and marked the beginning of the Christmas season.

In the 1950s, the windows were very traditional with candy canes, Santas and ladies' mannequins wearing their formal attire and keeping warm with fur coats and jackets while surrounding a life-size horse and carriage in the snow. Most years something new and different would be added or changed so shoppers could look forward to that year's holiday season at Famous-Barr. A fine example was publicized on November 30, 1982, in an article that ran in the *St. Louis Globe-Democrat.* Marcus Tully

The streets are filled with Christmas shoppers at the intersection of Seventh and Locust Streets outside Downtown Famous-Barr, 1960. *Courtesy of Missouri History Museum.*

II, the senior vice-president of marketing, announced, "Everything is new; from the garlands across the first floor ceilings, to the Christmas trees above the elevators, to Santa's spaceship in the corner window of 7th and Olive Streets." In the same article, Famous-Barr president Richard L. Battram stated, "Santaland will be called Santa's Spacework this year." The display featured a space-age family doing some old-fashioned Christmas baking. The new concept worked and drew people to the downtown store. The Christmas magic was back.

Business had been tough downtown for several years, and the St. Louis Centre Mall would not be constructed for a few years. Famous-Barr wanted shoppers to know it was committed to keeping the downtown store looking bright and interesting. Tully declared, "We will not abandon the Downtown Famous-Barr Flagship Store."

Many customers have holiday memories of going to take a picture with Santa Claus at Famous-Barr. In the early years through the 1960s, there were only white Santas. After the 1960s civil rights movement, things changed, and Famous-Barr hired its first black Santa. Now patrons had a choice of which Santa they wanted to take their picture with.

Linda LaDon Petersen is telling Santa Claus what she wants for Christmas at Downtown Famous-Barr Santaland, 1959. *Courtesy of Rusty Werner.*

In the late 1970s through most of the 1980s, there were five Santa booths set up in the Downtown Famous-Barr. The day after Thanksgiving, Christmas music was broadcast in the street outside the store. The songs got shoppers in the holiday mood and reminded them it was time to start shopping for gifts. While the grown-ups couldn't wait to see what was new this holiday, the children were anxious to discuss their Christmas wishes with Santa Claus.

Year after year, Famous-Barr kept the old holiday traditions and added new ones to keep people coming back to shop at Famous-Barr. In 1975, Joan Van de Erve was a Famous-Barr vice-president and publicity director. That year Santa Claus arrived at four branch stores in the Famous-Barr and KMOX traffic helicopter with Officer Don Miller. Santa arrived on November 22 at Northland, Northwest Plaza, Southtown and South County Famous-Barr. Two of the Santas were picked up at the old terminal at Lambert Field, one at Archery Range West of the Planetarium in Forest Park and the fourth at the Lindbergh High School athletic field.

On December 6, 1964, Famous-Barr held a Twenty-fifth Annual Christmas Party for children. The party included a special showing of the Walt Disney movie *Mary Poppin,* at Loew's State Theatre at 715 Washington

Crowds of Christmas shoppers rush to find the gifts on their holiday lists on Seventh Street outside Downtown Famous Barr, 1964. *Courtesy of Missouri History Museum.*

Avenue. The party drew over three thousand children and adults. To manage the crowd, Famous-Barr provided entertainment while groups of people got seated. The entertainment in the theater included sing-a-longs, clowns, baton twirlers and an accordion and organ player. Mr. Stanley Goodman, president of Famous-Barr, welcomed the audience, and then Santa Claus got on the stage to remind the children he had a gift, candy and a coloring book for each of them. In the 1960s, children could still be enticed to be on their best behavior in the presence of Santa Claus and sit through announcements and a movie respectfully.

In the 1970s, with the opening of indoor malls, the business climate downtown changed. Famous-Barr, along with the other department stores had to come up with new ideas to keep people interested in shopping downtown.

In 1973, the Downtown Famous-Barr windows were the stage for real live bears. The backdrop walls were painted in holiday colors, featuring

Passersby stop to admire the Christmas window at Downtown Famous-Barr, 1964. *Courtesy of Missouri History Museum.*

a fireplace with a roaring fire, a grandfather clock and a portrait of Mr. and Mrs. Bear hanging on the wall. A trainer worked with the bears, which performed tricks and were rewarded with treats. This live bear window created a lot more excitement from passersby than another window in the 1970s depicting stuffed bears on ice skates in a white winter wonderland, complete with a mirrored pond.

Before the 1970s, window and interior Christmas displays featuring basic toys were enough to entice grown-ups and children to Santaland at Famous-Barr. For decades, the customary toys created excitement during the holidays, but by the 1970s, basic and traditional needed a new twist.

An article that ran in the *St. Louis Globe-Democrat* on November 17, 1972, announced, "Ann, Andy and Santa Claus Are All Coming to Town." On the same day, the *St. Louis Post-Dispatch* published an article titled, "Top Doll in Santaland," which told the story of a nineteen-foot Raggedy Ann doll the Famous-Barr carpenters had made for this year's Santaland. Another article that ran in the *St. Louis Post-Dispatch* on December 1, 1972, stated the Famous-Barr Santaland was a "whirling and flashing mechanical fun factory." The theme this year was the "Wonderful World of Raggedy Ann and Andy." This year, the day-after-Thanksgiving tradition of making a trip to St. Louis downtown to view the holiday window displays and walk through Santaland in the Famous-Barr auditorium had a surprise. An oversize doll was the center of attention among the dozens of animated Raggedy Ann and Andy characters. The children attending the Christmas party at Downtown Famous-Barr were in awe of the giant Raggedy Ann in the Toy Factory.

In 1983, Downtown Famous-Barr advertised "All New Christmas Bearland." An article found in the Famous-Barr Public Relations Scrapbook begins, "Join in the Beary-Merry Christmas fun Downtown at Famous Barr today from 10 a.m. to 6 p.m." The article goes on to invite everyone to come out to the ninth-floor Santaland, where they would be greeted by the Famous Christmas Bears and a very wise and old tree. The article encouraged people to walk through the green forest and watch the bears working with Santa: "Meet Mr. Bigbear, who sits atop Magic Mountain." No doubt it was a delight to walk through Santaland for the children as well as their parents.

The store had plenty of bears in stock to sell, but the buzz for this year was Cabbage Patch Kids dolls. Shoppers stood in line to purchase these must-have dolls, sometimes waiting for hours only to find out the dolls were sold out. Some parents acted like children, fighting to grab one of the dolls when they were put on shelves. It was a sad Christmas for the kids who did not find the Cabbage Patch Kids doll they had asked for under the tree.

The holiday window display at Downtown Famous-Barr shows off party dresses and accessories for the 1987 season. *Courtesy of Missouri History Museum.*

They had specially asked for this doll while visiting Santa Claus in Bearland at Famous-Barr.

The late 1980s and 1990s brought about change in Famous-Barr's customers. While Downtown Famous-Barr continued to host mostly people who were window shopping and holding on to the tradition of walking through Santaland, the other Famous-Barr stores were appealing to shoppers who spent money. In 1991, at the Galleria, Chesterfield, West County and South County Famous-Barr locations, Charles Thorndike came to St. Louis for the first time for a signing event. According to the Annalee Sue Coffee website, "In the year 1990, Annalee Dolls became the headgear sponsor for Christopher Peterson, a member of the United States Ski Team." Charles Thorndike is an artist and the son of Chip and Annalee Davis Thorndike. Charles's mother was the original creator of the Annalee felt-covered dolls.

Also part of the 1991 holiday events was designer and master glassmaker Tihomir Tomic. He was in St. Louis for a crystal signing and sale event at the Galleria, South County, Downtown, Mid-Rivers, Northwest and St. Clair Famous-Barr stores. The most exclusive Christmas event at Famous-Barr was an appearance by Theo Faberge. Theo was the grandson of the Russian Imperial jeweler, Carl Faberge. During the holiday season of 1991, the Faberge St. Petersburg Collection was exclusively available in St. Louis at the Galleria Famous-Barr.

Also leading the Galleria Famous-Barr into the 1991 holiday season was an appearance by Paloma Picasso in October. Paloma was promoting her fragrances and handbags.

From 1988 to 1992, the Famous Bear costumes were designed by David and Donna Parks of Finale Costumes Inc. Peter "Juno" Hernandez Jr. was the Famous Bear for all Christmas events and promotions, and one year he also appeared in an Easter and St. Patrick's Day Parade.

In 1988, Sandy LaRouche created the character of the Snow Queen when she was employed by Famous-Barr. She took part in Famous-Barr's Santaland and Breakfast with Santa that year and also took part in other Christmas activities in St. Louis, like the Christmas parade. For five years, Sandy appeared as the Snow Queen at the Famous-Barr Breakfast with Santa. She continued as the Snow Queen of St. Louis off and on until 2011, appearing in the St. Louis First Night celebration and in parades.

The tradition of Christmas at Downtown Famous-Barr dated back to 1911. In the past, it had attracted over 100,000 visitors each year, but in 1991, Santaland was suffering. The ninth-floor auditorium where Santaland had been set up year after year was under construction. The

Peter Hernandez Jr., in the Famous Bear costume, waves to shoppers while he stands beside the Downtown Famous-Barr window display in 1988. *Courtesy of Missouri History Museum.*

May Department Stores Company was expanding its office space, and there would no longer be an auditorium. This year, photos with Santa would be taken on the fifth floor. Times were changing. Santa gave out live pine seedlings to the children who came by the store to visit him instead of handing out the traditional gifts of toys and coloring books that had been given out in the past. A memo found in the archives titled "Santaland Was a Disaster" gives us a clue of the 1991 holiday season. The memo starts, "The day after Thanksgiving, 95 percent of the customers were furious because we did not have the ninth-floor auditorium Bearland." Customers complained about having to pay downtown parking when they could just go to the mall, park for free and see the same thing. While some things changed, others stayed the same.

In 1992, Famous Barr and the American Flyer S Gaugers of the St. Louis area operated a model train for the fifth consecutive year. The model train was displayed in the Downtown Famous-Barr store windows at Seventh and Locust. Four trains operated continuously from 8:30 a.m. to 9:30 p.m. during the Christmas season. Joining the trains were a mine tram, a Cliffside train, two chairlifts, a streetcar, a coal lift and oil derricks. The layout required more than three hundred feet of track and used more than four hundred square feet of surface for the multilevel display.

Famous-Barr had promotions throughout the year, but the biggest percentage of its events took place during the holiday selling season. Helen Weiss, the divisional vice-president of public relations and special events, was interviewed by Gary Belsky in the *St. Louis Business Journal* in June 1985. Helen said, "Timing is key in planning special events." At this time, a staff of three people oversaw about 250 promotional events each year. These events included appearances and book signings, store grand-opening parties and Christmas walk-throughs. According to Weiss, "75 percent of the Famous-Barr special events are merchandising promotions. The other 25 percent are for service/charity causes."

After months of going through the Famous-Barr archives, I came to the conclusion that there was always something exciting going on at Famous-Barr.

Chapter 5

FAMOUS PEOPLE AT FAMOUS

Celebrity Events and Promotions

It's Showtime at Famous!
—advertising in the St. Louis Post-Dispatch, *March 13, 1987*

Before the age of computers and shopping online, the best way to increase sales volume was to get a crowd of shoppers into a store. This crowd, in turn, created excitement and brought about a festive atmosphere, which got shoppers to spend money. But even if you didn't spend any money, the experience was an adventure to remember.

For many of us, Famous-Barr was the place where we saw for the first time a movie star, a star athlete, an Olympic gold medalist, a professional model, a New York designer or a national author. The best part was that we didn't have to travel to see such celebrities, and the events were free of charge. The public relations, marketing and visual merchandising staffs at Famous-Barr brought in the "Famous People" and set the stage for us to meet and admire them and—in most cases—buy the product they represented.

The first color television in St. Louis was featured at the Downtown Famous-Barr in 1956. It was an exciting time in the city and at Famous-Barr. To celebrate, Morton D. "Buster" May, chief executive officer of the May Department Stores Company, welcomed St. Louis mayor Raymond R. Tucker, Red Schoendienst and Stan Musial to take part in this historical event in St. Louis. Mayor Raymond R. Tucker was the mayor in St. Louis from 1953 to 1965. Red Schoendienst was signed by the St. Louis Cardinals as an amateur free agent in 1942. Red played for the Cardinals, Braves and

Mayor Tucker, Buster May, Red Schoendienst and Stan Musial were at Downtown Famous-Barr celebrating the arrival of the first color televisions to be sold in St. Louis in 1956. *Courtesy of Missouri History Museum.*

the Giants from 1945 to 1963. He was inducted into the Baseball Hall of Fame in 1989. Stan "the Man" Musial was signed by the St. Louis Cardinals as an amateur free agent in 1938. Stan played with the Cardinals from 1941 to 1963. He was inducted into the Baseball Hall of Fame in 1969 and died in 2013 at the age of ninety-two.

Buster May had an interest in art, literature, sports, food and music. His interests were a big advantage for St. Louis citizens. Through events and promotions, May brought in some of the most interesting Americans to St. Louis and Famous-Barr. In June 1956, there were appearances by Vaughn Monroe and Mary McCarty. In the 1940s and 1950s, Monroe was a popular singer, musician, big band leader and an actor. He earned two stars on the Hollywood Walk of Fame; one was awarded for recording, the other one for radio. McCarty was an author, critic and political activist who wrote twenty-eight books during her lifetime. In 1955 she wrote the book called *A Charmed Life*.

Bob Gibson is signing autographs at Downtown Famous-Barr to promote his first book written with Phil Pepe, *From Ghetto to Glory*, in 1968. *Courtesy of Missouri History Museum.*

Celebrities weren't brought in just to promote products or books; they also made appearances at Famous-Barr new store openings. The new store at South County Shopping Center opened in August 1963. It was summer, and summer in America means baseball, and baseball in St. Louis means the Cardinals. The best personalities to encourage shoppers to come and check out the new store were two baseball stars. St. Louis Cardinals third baseman Ken Boyer and shortstop Dick Groat made an appearance and signed autographs for the customers who came out for the store's grand opening.

Bob Gibson signed his first book written with Phil Pepe, *From Ghetto to Glory*, in the book department at the downtown store in 1968. That year, he was a pitcher for the St. Louis Cardinals and was making baseball history with his record-breaking performance. Gibson became the first pitcher to strike out thirty-five players in a single World Series game. He was named the 1968 National League's MVP and honored with the Cy Young Award the same year. In 1981, Gibson was inducted into the Baseball Hall of Fame.

Another star athlete to make an appearance at the downtown store in 1968 was Carol Heiss, a 1960 Olympic gold medalist figure skater. Heiss's appearance was part of the Beautiful American event. Years later, Adidas sportswear would bring in another Olympic gold medalist, Jackie Joyner-Kersee, to Famous-Barr. Joyner-Kersee, the three-times Olympic gold medalist, is a St. Louis local. In 1980, she graduated high school in East St. Louis, Illinois. In 2004, she was inducted into the USA Track & Field Hall of Fame.

The year 1968 was an exciting one at Famous-Barr. Its events brought in the crowds, especially the Beautiful American event. One of the features during the event was the Wild West Show. For this show, Montie Montana Jr. and his trained horse Buck, along with two Pueblo Indians, made an appearance. At that time, Montana was an actor, stuntman, trick rider, roper and rodeo performer. His father, Montie Montana, was also an actor and rodeo personality who appeared in several movies with John Wayne.

Sophia Loren was at the Downtown and the Northwest stores in their cosmetic departments in the fall of 1980 to introduce her perfume, Sophia, by Coty. To kick off the event, there was a cocktail party at the Old Warsaw.

Sophia Loren is peering into the window display at Downtown Famous-Barr announcing her appearance to promote Sophia, by Coty, in 1980. *Courtesy of Missouri History Museum.*

The guests included executives of the May Department Stores Company headquarters in St. Louis, and invitations were sent to executives at other St. Louis–area companies, including Venture and Sears in St. Ann, Super X in Maryland Heights, J.C. Penney, Walgreens, Woolco, Glaser and Schnuck's. The Coty Company personnel were invited, along with Missouri governor Joseph Teasdale, St. Louis mayor James Conway and their wives.

On September 30, there was a private dinner in honor of Sophia Loren aboard the *Robert E. Lee*. Members of the press were invited to take pictures, but they were not granted invitations to the dinner—or that was what the local media thought. They found out different when Richard Weiss shared Bill McClellan's Sophia story, which ran in the *St. Louis Post-Dispatch* on October 31, 2007. The article was titled "Unforgettable Interviews: When Harry Met Sophia." When Sophia came to St. Louis, Harry Levins was a city editor. He knew Helen Weiss at Famous-Barr well, but he would never ask for a special favor—that is, until Sophia Loren came to town. Levins called Weiss, who was in charge of Famous-Barr public relations and promotions, and said, "I'll be forever in your debt if I could meet Sophia Loren. I'll do anything. If there's a double axe murder at Famous, I'll bury it."

According to the story, there was only one ticket allotted for the newspaper, and it wasn't for Levins, it was for *St. Louis Post-Dispatch* reporter John McGuire. To Levins's benefit, Helen did manage to come up with a second ticket. But there was another gentleman in the St. Louis media who wanted to see the most beautiful woman in the world, and that was Julius Hunter at KMOX. KMOX had already missed the promotional activities, and Hunter's bosses were not around. So Hunter took matters into his own hands and called Helen Weiss, saying, "I'll be forever in your debt..." Helen came through and asked Hunter to get to the *Robert E. Lee* right away, telling him he could interview Sophia before dinner.

Levins and McGuire were already there; they had arrived early and had a few glasses of wine. They would have drunk beer, but none had been offered, so they drank the wine in the same matter they drank their beer, which made them a little tipsy. Hunter and his camera crew got to the boat, and Helen set them up in a small room where they could watch Sophia step out of the limousine. Hunter reminisces, "It was like the movies: the car door was opened, and this leg came out. It just kept coming." Hunter ended up escorting Loren into the dining room; after the interview, Helen had asked him if he would mind.

Meanwhile, Levins and McGuire were seated at a table close to where Loren was sitting. At the end of her meal, she wiped her mouth lightly with a napkin, and conveniently—that is, for Levins—she dropped the napkin under the table before she left. Levins couldn't let the opportunity get away, so he crawled on the floor under the table and went home with a souvenir. After all these years, Levins still has the napkin with the lip prints of the most

French actress and dancer Marine Jahan is modeling Nine West shoes at Chesterfield Famous-Barr in 1985. *Courtesy of Missouri History Museum.*

beautiful woman in the world. Bill McClellan ended the article by saying, "Loren celebrated her 73rd birthday last month. Being guys, Levins and Hunter are still 15."

Another voluptuous movie star came to Famous-Barr in 1982. Lana Turner appeared in the book department at the Downtown and Clayton

In 1983, Erma Bombeck signed her first book, *At Wit's End*, which was published in 1965, at West Park Mall Famous-Barr in Cape Girardeau. *Courtesy of Missouri History Museum.*

stores to promote her book, *Lana: The Lady, the Legend, the Truth*. From 1937 to 1980, Turner starred in numerous movies. Her last work in film was from 1982 to 1983 in the TV series *Falcon Crest*. She played Jacqueline Perrault. Turner officially retired from acting in 1983, and she died in 1995.

Marine Jahan is a French dancer and actress who is best known in the United States for being Jennifer Beals's double in the 1983 movie *Flashdance*. In 1984, she was cast as a dancer in *Streets of Fire*, and in *It's Flashbeagle, Charlie Brown*, she was a performance model for the "Snoopy Dance."

Erma Bombeck, an American humorist, came to Famous-Barr in 1987 to promote her book *Family: The Ties that Bind...and Gag!* By this time, she was already well known for her newspaper columns in which she wrote about

Elaine Viets was at Famous-Barr on September 23, 1987, to promote her upcoming book, *Urban Affairs*. *Courtesy of Missouri History Museum.*

suburban home life. She had been to the Cape Girardeau Famous-Barr in 1983 to promote her book *At Wit's End*. Her career, spanning from 1965 to 1996, produced fifteen books and over four thousand newspaper columns. She died in 1996.

In 1988, Elaine Viets, St. Louis' own columnist from the *St. Louis Post-Dispatch*, made an appearance at Downtown Famous Barr in the Viking Room on the sixth floor. The event, "Let's Do Lunch," was to promote her upcoming first book, *Urban Affairs: Tales from the Heart of the City*. Viets grew up in South St. Louis and currently resides in South Florida. She is best known for her *Dead-End* series of books, which involve solving a mystery to find the murderer. The series include *Shop Till You Drop*, *Murder Between the Covers*, *Dying to Call You*, *Just Murdered* and *Murder Unleashed*.

Today if you want or need a wig you can buy one online, look for one at a mall kiosk or shop in a wig shop. If you were shopping for wigs in the 1980s, you could find one at Famous-Barr. Its premier line was Eva Gabor Wigs. So it is no surprise that on May 11, 1988, Eva Gabor herself made a personal appearance at the downtown store. People from all walks of life came in to see Miss Gabor—not to be fitted for a wig but to see "Lisa Douglas," Gabor's accented absent-minded blonde bombshell character in the TV series *Green Acres*, which aired from 1965 to 1971.

Kaye Lani Rae Rafko won the title of Miss America 1988. In November, she came to St. Louis for an appearance at the Famous-Barr West County store opening. Rafko went on to marry Charles Wilson, and they have three children. They reside in Monroe, Michigan, where Kaye works as an oncology nurse. She enjoys being a community leader and still goes around the country on speaking engagements.

Cicely Tyson was at the Famous-Barr Northwest reopening on November 9, 1989. Tyson was raised in New York City and started her career as a model when she was discovered by *Ebony* magazine. Her acting career began in 1957 in off-Broadway productions, and she also played small roles in feature films. Her first major role was in the movie *The Heart Is a Lonely Hunter*. In 1972, Cicely was nominated for an Academy Award for Best Actress for her role in *Sounder*. In 1974, she played the role of a former slave in *The Autobiography of Miss Jane Pittman*. She won two Emmy Awards for this role. Tyson was in the television miniseries *Roots* in 1977 in which she played Binta, the mother of Kunta Kinte. In 1978, she was in the miniseries *King* and *A Woman Called Moses*. In 1997, she was awarded a star on the Hollywood Walk of Fame.

Donna Fujii started her image consulting business in San Francisco in 1978. In 1989, she conducted a fashion seminar at Famous-Barr in the Petites

Cicely Tyson made an appearance at the Famous-Barr Northwest reopening on November 9, 1989. *Courtesy of Missouri History Museum.*

Department. Her consultations are based on color analysis for people who want to improve their self-image. Based on your skin tone and hair coloring, the seminar gave direction on what colors to wear to harmonize your wardrobe and makeup. She also recommended which colors and styles to wear according to a person's body type and style personality. In 1990, Fujii published her book *Color With Style.*

In the 1980s, the aerobic craze took root after Richard Simmons and Jane Fonda discovered fitness was big business. In the early 1990s, aerobics exercise was still popular, and department stores around the country featured aerobic shops in their stores. Famous-Barr was no different and even kicked it up a notch. L.A. Gear, a manufacturer of fitness clothes and athletic shoes, brought in Gil Janklowicz for an appearance. Janklowicz, the L.A. Gear spokesperson and host of ESPN's *Bodies in Motion*, did an aerobic demonstration, signed autographs and gave exercise tips.

On August 12, 1991, Elizabeth Taylor was at the Galleria store promoting her new fragrance, White Diamonds. The customers who purchased a one-ounce bottle of White Diamonds for $300 got to meet Elizabeth Taylor. The sales associate who sold the most one-ounce bottles of the fragrance won a diamond pendant necklace. Shirley Barken sold the most bottles and got the necklace and the chance to meet and visit with Miss Taylor.

Shirley Barken started her career at the store in Clayton in 1957. When the Clayton Famous-Barr closed, she went to work at the new store in the Galleria. Shirley is still working for Macy's at the St. Louis Galleria in the Fragrance Department. She has always loved her work, and she has numerous awards to show for it. Throughout her career, Shirley Barken has been tops in sales. In an article that ran in the March 1994 *Beauty Fashion Publication*,

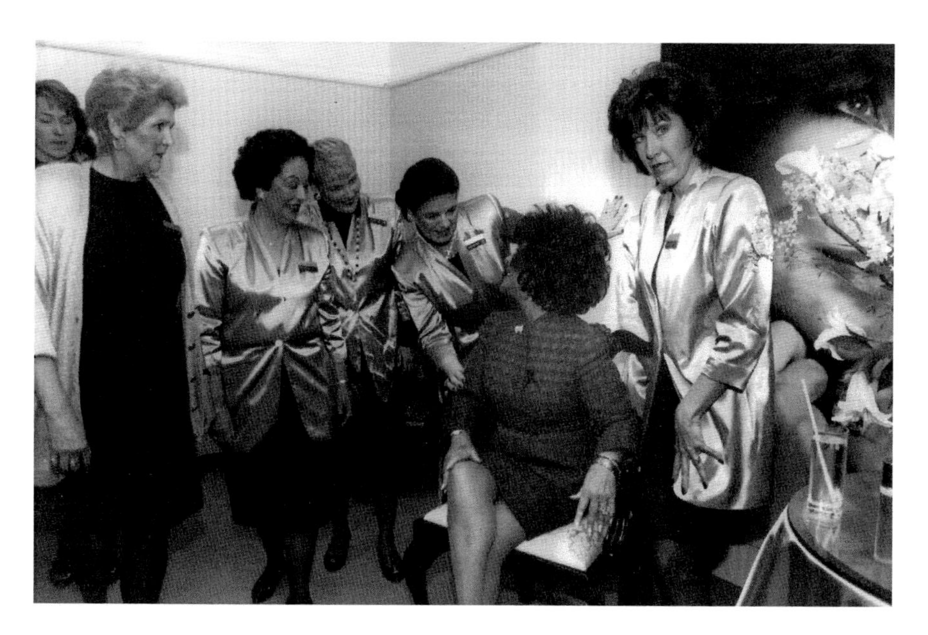

Shirley Barken, third from left, and a few of her fellow employees met Elizabeth Taylor at the Galleria Famous-Barr for the launch of White Diamonds in 1991. *Courtesy of Shirley Barken.*

Shirley was featured as a beauty advisor for Riviera Concepts at Famous-Barr. At that time, she had been with Famous-Barr for thirty-seven years and had surpassed every selling standard set for her by the company. She was already a member of the exclusive President's Club for over-achieving her sales quotas and in 1991 had served as its president. The article read, "She never feels badly about going to work and enjoys the excitement of meeting new people every day."

By 1994, Shirley had worked for twenty-five different department managers and had been offered the department manager's position several times. But being in management was not what Shirley aspired to. Shirley enjoys helping her customers make their purchases, and it shows. She has won the honor of "Selling Star" for having the highest productivity in cosmetics and fragrances and has also won a "Diamond Star," the highest customer service award a beauty advisor can attain at Famous-Barr.

Shirley attributes her success to knowing her customers and being flexible to change. She believes it's harder to sell to today's more sophisticated customers. In the days before researching a product on the Internet, clients relied solely on Shirley's recommendations as the expert on a product. Today, even though research can be done on computers before making a

Kathie Lee Gifford was at Galleria Famous-Barr promoting her clothing line Kathie Lee for Plaza South in 1992. *Courtesy of Missouri History Museum.*

purchase, customers still trust Shirley and take her advice as they have for years. Proof of customers listening to her sales advice is in a letter sent to Shirley by the Regional Sales Manager for Ralph Lauren fragrances. The letter is dated February 13, 1995, and it was sent to congratulate her on winning the Beauty Sales Award for Safari Women. There is a line that reads, "It is a pleasure to have you represent us and I also congratulate you on being a 6 Time Winner!"

Kathie Lee Gifford was at the Galleria Famous-Barr in March 1992. At this time, Kathie Lee Gifford was a co-host on *Live with Regis and Kathie Lee*. An article stated, "If Kathie Lee Gifford were running for president, she couldn't have kissed more babies, shaken more hands and posed for more snapshots with well-wishers than she did Saturday afternoon at the Galleria." The article went on to say that several thousand of Gifford's fans came out for the introduction of the new Kathie Lee for Plaza South line of clothing. Gifford appeared after a fashion show in which models showed off dresses from her line. She was greeted by a very enthusiastic crowd that cheered as the flashbulbs went off. When someone in the crowd shouted out, "Sing for us!" She sang a few lines from, "Meet Me in St. Louis."

After the show, Kathie Lee stood for more than an hour and a half while fans came by for autographed photos, hugs and snapshots. St. Louisans just loved her and her generosity. Her appearance fee was donated to the St. Louis Chapter of the Variety Club, and part of the proceeds from her clothing line sales went to charities.

The following month there was another big name at the Galleria Famous-Barr: designer Oscar de la Renta. Shoppers were invited to come meet de la Renta while he was promoting his new fragrance, Volupte, available exclusively at Famous-Barr.

Two well-known celebrities who also appeared at Famous-Barr in the 1990s were Fabio in 1993 and Vanna White in 1995. Fabio, the male Italian supermodel, is best known as the face and body on the cover of hundreds of romance novels from the 1980s and 1990s. Vanna White is best known as the co-host of the television game show *Wheel of Fortune*. She was at Famous-Barr Galleria as part of "Bed Bank," a program that donated mattresses to homeless shelters. The event was sponsored by Spring Air's St. Louis factory and Famous-Barr.

Former St. Louis Cardinals catcher Tim McCarver made a personal appearance at the Galleria store in May 2005. He was promoting his book *Few and Chosen: Defining Cardinal Greatness Across Eras*. McCarver wrote the book with Phil Pepe. Tim McCarver was a catcher in the major leagues for twenty-one seasons. He played with the St. Louis Cardinals for eleven years and played in two World Series championships. After his baseball career, he turned to broadcasting, working for Joe Buck as a baseball analyst for the Fox Network.

Other "Famous People at Famous" who made appearances at the stores included fashion designers Tommy Hilfiger and Carole Little; fashion retailer and entrepreneur Fred Hayman, the founder of Giorgio Beverly Hills; and Robin Leach, producer, host and writer of the television series *Lifestyles of the Rich and Famous*. Leach was brought in to promote the fragrance Red, by Giorgio Beverly Hills. Kelly Bevan, a *Vogue* editor, and Edward Cortese, an associate editor and official spokesperson for *GQ* magazine, both made appearances at the stores. Academy Award–winning actress Joan Fontaine, actor/comedian Rip Taylor and movie star Debbie Reynolds were all at Famous-Barr for events in 1984. Wally Amos, the creator of Famous Amos chocolate chip cookies, also made an appearance. Even psychic and intuitive Tori Hartman came to Famous-Barr. Isaac Bruce, St. Louis Rams football star, was in the men's department at the Galleria for a personal appearance and to sign autographs.

While clothing designers made store appearances to promote their product lines, the manufacturers for Famous-Barr brought in athletic stars to promote their brands. In 1993, Olympic gold medalists Bart Conner and Nadia Comaneci made personal appearances at the Galleria store for Jockey International, Inc. Haggar, the men's clothing manufacturer sponsored appearances by St. Louis Cardinals Tom Pagnozzi and Milt Thompson. The Arrow brand of men's clothing sponsored appearances by St. Louis Cardinals Rex "Hurricane" Hudler and Ozzie Smith.

St. Louis Cardinals shortstop Ozzie Smith was one of the celebrities with the most appearances in the history of Famous-Barr. In 1985, he was on the main floor in the remodeled Downtown Famous-Barr signing his photographs for the Karl Lagerfeld Fan Collection. In 1987, Ozzie drew a crowd of about 1,500 at the West County Famous-Barr as part of Arrow Company's Arrow All-Star Team '87 Best Dressed Athletes. Two hundred units of the VHS movie *Ozzie the Movie* were shipped to sell during the event. Another member of the Arrow's team in 1987 was St. Louis Cardinals second baseman Tommy Herr. On November 9, 1988, Ozzie Smith shared the spotlight with Cicely Tyson at the Famous-Barr Northwest reopening.

There are so many more celebrities and famous personalities who made appearances at Famous-Barr. The ones mentioned are some of the names found in the archives department at the Missouri History Museum Library and Research Center in the Famous-Barr Publicity Department Records. During the era of big-dollar events and promotions, you just never knew what famous person you might run into at Famous-Barr.

Chapter 6

COMMUNITY SERVICE

St. Louis Events Sponsored by Famous-Barr

Morton J. May, noted St. Louis merchant and philanthropist, has been named winner of the 1966 Humanities award presented by the St. Louis Globe Democrat.

—The Global Jewish News Source, *January 13, 1967*

Famous-Barr, owned by the May Department Stores Company, was about community service since the early days of doing business. The earliest community service reference found was a lecture at the downtown auditorium given by Dr. Minnie Finkon on April 9, 1915. The lecture was titled "Style and Health."

The company's focus on community service also included activities for the Famous-Barr employees. The business understood the benefits of happy and healthy workers. The Famous-Barr Farm on the Meramec River opened June 23, 1912. It was a place owned by the company where it sponsored outings for their employees. In 1915, the employees of Famous-Barr held their Annual River Excursion on the *Grey Eagle* boat that set sail from the foot of Olive Street. The excursion was an evening event set for 8:00 p.m. For the younger employees, the company planned a two-day outing at the Famous-Barr Farm. The outing included adult chaperones.

The company encouraged music and sports. In 1916, there was a Famous-Barr Band that gave concerts in Eureka, Missouri. For those who played tennis, the company sponsored its Annual Tennis Contest for employees in 1917.

In 1969, this booklet was given to the students who signed up for the Famous-Barr Camelot Gourmet Cooking School, organized by Margie May to raise money for charity. *Courtesy of Manfred P. Zettl.*

In 1969, Famous-Barr executive chef Manfred P. Zettl taught the Camelot Gourmet Cooking School. The school was offered to St. Louis society ladies to raise money for charities. The classes were organized by Margie May, wife of Morton D. May. The twelve ladies in the class would learn to cook one recipe a week. The last week of the school the husbands were invited to dine with their spouses and enjoy their wives' culinary creations.

Morton and Margie May were great patrons of the arts. For years, Famous-Barr held the Gypsy Caravan in the Famous-Barr parking lots of suburban shopping centers. In 1964, Joan Van de Erve, vice-president and publicity director at Famous-Barr, called the Gypsy Caravan "one of the world's biggest outdoor antique fairs." More than four hundred exhibitors took part in 1973. The caravan featured antiques, arts and crafts for sale to benefit the St. Louis Symphony.

The Fourth of July celebration events sponsored by Famous-Barr on the Riverfront were legendary. They started out in 1964 as Famous-Barr's Annual Independence Day Water and Sky Spectacle on the Riverfront. The

The fireworks display above the Gateway Arch for the Bicentennial Festival drew big crowds along the Mississippi River in 1976. *Courtesy of Missouri History Museum.*

In 1987, the runners at the 10K Annual Gateway Run in Downtown St. Louis picked up their racing packets at the Downtown Famous-Barr, where the awards ceremony took place after the race. *Courtesy of Missouri History Museum.*

event took place every year from 1964 to 1978. The festival involved water and sky events, but it was the fireworks display that drew the largest crowds to the Mississippi River Riverfront and Gateway Arch.

In 1976, there was a request made for an AV-8A aircraft for a flight demonstration for the St. Louis 4th of July Festival. At first it was denied but later reconsidered and approved, paving the way for the tradition of the Fair St. Louis Air Show.

In the 1970s, there was a running boom in America. Millions of people were jogging for recreation and fitness, while others were running to compete. There were races sponsored around the country. From 1979 to 1988, Famous-Barr was one of the major sponsors of the 10K Annual Gateway Run.

Sandy LaRouche worked in public relations with Helen Weiss from August 1, 1978, to July 4, 1989. Sandy was the special events coordinator and the assistant public relations director. She recalls some of the other sponsors of the Gateway Run as Runner Up, Swatch, Playtex, Jockey and Nike. She remembers over one thousand runners taking part in the 10K race, which was listed as, "One of the 100 Great American Road Races" by *Runner Magazine*. The registered runners picked up their T-shirts and race packets at Downtown Famous-Barr. The winners were awarded some great prizes donated by store merchants and the sponsors. These prizes were awarded in the downtown Famous-Barr store at the awards ceremonies, where the after-race festivities took place in the ninth-floor auditorium.

Sandy adds, "We also produced a half-marathon called the Sunrise Scramble. The races were put on with the assistance of Jerry Kokesh of Marathon Sports and the St. Louis Track Club." Besides sponsoring runs, Famous-Barr also sponsored walks. In 1988, the Zoo's Annual Fall Walk was presented by the Zoo Friends Association and sponsored by Famous-Barr and Reebok.

The National Senior Games Association initially known as the National Senior Olympics Organization started in 1985 in St. Louis, Missouri, with a group of seven men and women. The organization promotes healthy lifestyles for men and women over fifty years of age. It provides an opportunity for seniors to compete in sports and social events. The event is held annually over the Memorial Day weekend and attracts more than one thousand athletes to participate in ninety events.

In 1989, senior citizens danced to compete at the Silver Foxtrot Senior Olympics in front of a Famous-Barr store. *Courtesy of Missouri History Museum.*

The marching bands contest was part of the Freedom Festival of the V.P. Fair in the early 1990s. *Courtesy of Missouri History Museum.*

In 1987, St. Louis was the host for the first National Senior Olympic Games. The event attracted 2,500 competitors and over 100,000 spectators. The crowd was entertained by Bob Hope at the St. Louis Riverfront Arch. St. Louis hosted the event again in 1989, bringing in 3,500 senior competitors. This time there was national media coverage in the *New York Times*, as well as on *ESPN* and *Good Morning America.* The thirty-fifth annual St. Louis Senior Olympics took place May 22–27, 2014.

Older Adult Service and Information System (OASIS), a nonprofit organization, was founded in St. Louis in 1982. The organization provides educational, cultural and wellness opportunities through lectures, seminars and classes for people who are over the age of sixty. In 1990, OASIS was sponsored by the May Department Stores Company, Famous-Barr, the Jewish Hospital of St. Louis and Washington University School of Medicine. Since its founding in 1982, May Department Stores provided space for some of OASIS's programs. In 1985, OASIS had centers at Famous-Barr stores in Northland Shopping Center, Southtown and Clayton.

According to the Veiled Prophet Organization, the Freedom Festival of the Veiled Prophet Fair Parade is "Saint Louis' grandest parade since 1878." It has become part of Fair St. Louis. For over thirty years, the parade had

Models wore the latest dress designs at Clayton Famous-Barr for the *Vogue Magazine* Grand Style Fashion Show to benefit Grand Center in 1990. *Courtesy of Missouri History Museum.*

been held downtown with celebrations along the banks of the Mississippi River and the surrounding grounds of the Gateway Arch. In 2014, the fair was held in Forest Park, the location of the 1904 World's Fair. Due to renovations at the Jefferson National Expansion Memorial, where the 630-foot Gateway Arch monument is the centerpiece, the location had to be moved from downtown. The celebration was promoted as the "Nation's Biggest Birthday Party."

A press release from the Veiled Prophet Organization dated October 23, 2013, stated there would be a parade featuring eighteen floats and over 750 performers in costumes. The High School Marching Bands Contest brings in "some of the greatest high school bands throughout the Midwest to compete for the 1776 Revolutionary War Snare Drum Traveling Trophy and over $10,000 in prizes." The festivities for 2014 were special, since this year marks the 250th birthday of St. Louis.

In 1990, there was a *Vogue* fashion show and cocktail party sponsored by Famous-Barr at Grand Center to benefit the Grand Center Organization, founded in 1981. The event was called "In Grand Style." Grand Center, in midtown St. Louis, is a center for cultural and entertainment activities. The Fox Theatre is the place to attend a concert or a Broadway musical. Powell Symphony Hall is the home of the St. Louis Symphony Orchestra. The Sheldon Concert Hall and Grandel Theatre are also located in this area. If it's jazz you're looking for at Grand Center, the place is Jazz at the Bistro. There are sixteen galleries and museums, and the radio stations of KWMU and KDHX relocated to the area to join other public media operations such as Nine Network, the *St. Louis Beacon* and Higher Education Channel (HEC-TV.) The area also houses secondary schools, such as Cardinal Ritter College Prep, Clyde C. Miller Career Academy and Loyola Academy. There is also an annual artistic circus by St. Louis' own Circus Flora. With its stage venues, restaurants, art spaces, festivals, celebrations and proximity to St. Louis University, Grand Center attracts over one million visitors annually.

In 1993, there was another *Vogue* fashion show to benefit the Children's Miracle Network at the Famous-Barr Galleria. The Children's Miracle Network Hospitals of Greater St. Louis is a nonprofit organization dedicated to raising funds and awareness for St. Louis Children's Hospital and SSM Cardinal Glennon Children's Medical Center. The money raised stays in St. Louis, helping the two hospitals to buy equipment, create new programs and make renovations to the facilities.

The medical community had also benefited from a fashion show in 1990, sponsored by Famous-Barr to benefit the Jewish Hospital School of Nursing Alumni Association. Starting in 1984, Famous-Barr hosted Heart House, sponsored by Alpha Phi sorority to benefit Children's Hospital for its Valentine's Day celebration. Famous-Barr provided the space to sell valentine crafts on consignment from artists in the St. Louis area. The fundraiser began at the West County store and later included the downtown store location.

Famous-Barr was a big part of the St. Louis Book Fair. According to an article that ran April 30, 1992, in the *St. Louis Post-Dispatch*, Famous-Barr was the sponsor for the Forty-third Annual Greater St. Louis Book Fair. The article gave a brief history of the book fair, stating, "It had started in the 1940s and was held at Temple Israel at 5017 Washington Avenue." The article went on to say that for twenty-eight years the book fair had been held in the parking lot of the Clayton Famous-Barr store. In 1992, the book sale to benefit the Nursery Foundation of St. Louis would be held in the West County Famous-Barr parking lot.

Fashion and food: Famous-Barr knew how to bring those two together to raise money for many different causes. On September 23, 1993, Famous-Barr and DKNY (Donna Karan New York) hosted an event to benefit the Aids Foundation of St. Louis at the Galleria store. An estimated four hundred guests were in attendance at the cocktail buffet.

In December 1993, Famous-Barr sponsored the Sheer Elegance Fashion Show and Luncheon Fundraiser to benefit the Boys' Club of St. Louis. The event was held at the Adam's Mark Hotel, at Fourth and Chestnut Streets. There is no longer an Adam's Mark; it is now the Hyatt Regency St. Louis Riverfront Hotel.

Famous-Barr cosmetic vendors and even a French crystal company could also be counted on to help with donations and fundraisers. In 1990, Famous-Barr asked its vendors for donations to the Missouri Botanical Garden for the reopening of the Climatron Gala; Liz Claiborne Cosmetics donated $5,000. That same year, Famous-Barr sponsored a fashion show for the Missouri Botanical Garden called Mothers and Daughters Show and Luncheon. In 2003, Evelyn Lauder, senior corporate vice-president for Estée Lauder, came to Famous-Barr West County. Ms. Lauder came to promote her book, *An Eye for Beauty*. All the book royalties went directly to the Breast Cancer Research Foundation. In 1990, Famous-Barr sent a check for $2,525 to the Missouri Historical Society from a Baccarat crystal promotion.

Other community services, which were good business for Famous-Barr, were bridal, prom beauty and back-to-school seminars. These seminars educated customers, who in turn bought products from the stores. Bridal and baby gift registries also provided an opportunity to help customers select the products they would need to set up a household or to prepare for the arrival of a new baby.

CHAPTER 7

MAJOR SALES EVENTS

FROM PARADES TO ART SHOWS

Look What We Have in Store for You This Month
—company tag line used in advertising for 1987

Famous-Barr was a St. Louis fashion leader and trendsetter from the beginning. In spring of 1913, crowds showed up at the store to view the latest in American and French designs. The event was advertised as the Fashion Fête. There was music, flowers and fashions to encourage shoppers to linger and forget about any troubles they might have. It was the perfect time to start thinking about social events and selecting the apparel to be worn after the dullness of winter. The exhibit encouraged shoppers to come see "what is fashion-approved for 1913." To entice the ladies, there were evening gowns, dresses for street use and daintier styles for parties. For the more conservative women, there were tailored suits and hats for every occasion. The accessories featured were made in America and in Europe. Jewelry, hair ornaments and neckwear were offered.

The ladies' fashions at this time required petticoats, corsets and hosiery; these, too, were offered. A lady of style also wanted her home to reflect the latest trends; for the home, there were rugs, linoleums, curtains, bedding and furniture. For customers who had their clothes made by tailors or seamstresses, there were plenty of fabrics, ribbons, laces and other trimmings to choose from.

The newest Famous-Barr opened in 1955 at Northland Shopping Center and featured the latest in appliances. The "latest" were more efficient

The fiberglass in appliances display at Northland Famous-Barr showcased the latest in appliances in 1955. *Courtesy of Missouri History Museum.*

appliances insulated with fiberglass. During the Jubilee Sales Event, these appliances went on sale. Philco Automatic refrigerators along with Caloric Ultramatic ranges were featured; the range had a regular price of $309.95 and was offered on sale for $249.95.

Frank Scheithauer, who worked for Famous-Barr from 1958 to 1995 in the Display Department, later known as Visual Merchandising, shared an interesting story handed down through oral history. In the early days before the big events at Famous-Barr, the company attracted customers into the store by providing excellent customer service. During the time gaslights were being replaced by electric lights in St. Louis homes, the store had a special area in the fabric department that featured both gas and electric lights. Customers were invited to look at the fabrics they were considering under gas lighting and then electric lighting; that way they could have a better idea how the fabrics were going to look under different lights.

The Clayton Famous-Barr opened in 1948 and was out to attract a more sophisticated customer, including world travelers and such. In 1961, the

In 1961, Marcel Toussaint and Odette Comer performed on stage at Clayton Famous-Barr for the "Bridges of Paris" production, a luncheon that was part of the Around the World event. *Courtesy of Marcel Toussaint.*

store had a series of six luncheons for its Around the World event. Each luncheon had a different theme based on different countries. One of the themes was "Bridges of Paris," which featured historic anecdotes narrated by Mrs. Richard B. Dempsey. Mrs. Dempsey was accompanied by a lute player for this French production. The production was directed by French teacher Marcel Toussaint and featured other St. Louis French teachers as well. The performers wore costumes from various periods in French history, which were custom-made by couturiers in France. Odette Comer, sister of Toussaint, also took part in this event.

The Fashion Junior and College Board members at Famous-Barr were the trendsetters at their high schools and universities. Cathy Frank Sherman tells us, "It was a prestigious thing to be on the board." Famous-Barr boasted having the largest Junior Department and even had its own fashion director until the early 1980s. The Fashion Junior and College Board was good business. An article printed on March 28, 1985, in the *St. Louis Post-Dispatch* gives us a better understanding of the Fashion Junior and College Board at Famous-Barr. The board consisted of thirty teenage girls who competed for the job. They had to be at least sixteen years of age, complete an application and provide photographs of themselves. The girls who were chosen would work as sales clerks in the Junior Department, model in fashion shows, assist with special events and work on community volunteer projects. These teenage girls were the expert fashionistas.

One of the largest events was Famous-Barr's Fashion Caravan fashion show in the 1960s. On August 12, 1963, the Famous-Barr South County store parking lot was the venue for this event. The fashion show featured college fashions, and the stage reflected the "flower power" ideals of the early 1960s in America. An article about the event read, "An ancient Fire Wagon and a Calliope will arrive on the scene, carrying the men's and women's College Boards of all Famous-Barr stores, who will model, sing and dance through the show." There were other trucks modeled after old circus wagons used for the event, and the truck trailers served as the models' dressing rooms.

When the Beatles were introduced to the United States on the *Ed Sullivan Show* in February 1964, it sparked an infatuation in America with all things

Famous-Barr's Fashion Caravan fashion show was held in the parking lot of the South County store in 1963. *Courtesy of Missouri History Museum.*

The exhibition and sale of African art held at Famous-Barr created excitement in St. Louis and attracted the local media in 1964. *Courtesy of Missouri History Museum.*

British. Famous-Barr saw an opportunity and promptly sent Sam Clark, its display director (Visual Merchandising Department), to England. Clark's job was to bring back the British look concept to St. Louis. The result was the Way-In Shop in the Famous-Barr Junior Department. The concept was "Way into fashion," in contrast to the popular phrase of the time, "Far out!" The Way-In Shop was groovy, and it featured black lighting on blue painted walls to achieve the psychedelic mood of the sixties. Famous-Barr, always the fashion leader, was the first department store in St. Louis to introduce bell-bottom jeans in the men's department in the late 1960s. Later, it was also the store that provided stylish clothes for the weather girl on Channel 5.

Morton "Buster" D. May was a great supporter of the arts, and Famous-Barr was a great avenue for him to share his love of art with the St. Louis community. Sometimes the art was on exhibit, and at other times it was for sale. The art ranged from artifacts to crafts. The earliest show mentioned in the Famous-Barr Publicity Department Records at the Missouri History Museum was the "Nepal Artifacts Show" in 1963. In May 1964, New Guinea art was on exhibit at the Clayton store. James Michener was brought in as a guest lecturer to talk about the art collection.

Also in 1964, Buster May would introduce St. Louis to the "Falling Man" series with the "Trova Exhibit." From 1964 to 1967, African art was featured and sold at Famous-Barr stores. In 1968, St. Louis artist Louis Bartig was at the store opening in Cape Girardeau as part of the grand-opening festivities. American painter Leroy Neiman displayed his art for the "Olympic Benefit Exhibition" at Famous-Barr in 1980. There was also an "Indian Exhibit" and an "Asian Exhibit" during the art years at Famous-Barr. Helen Weiss, who spent forty years with Famous-Barr in public relations, produced the art exhibits for Mr. May.

One of the most extravagant promotions at Famous-Barr was the Hail to the British Commonwealth on September 11–23, 1967. Most of the events took place at the Downtown store, but there were some special events that took place at the Clayton store penthouse. Downtown there were special exhibits and displays throughout the store. On the main floor was Miss Claude Kailer, collage maker. On the second floor, there was an Australian photo exhibit along with "Artists in Australia" and ships in bottles designed by craftsman Donald Gabbetis. The third-floor display and activities included an exhibit of a fifty-foot dragon boat from Hong Kong; greetings from Hong Kong children; an exhibit of Hong Kong children's artwork; an "Old and New Hong Kong" exhibit; the Art Needlework Workshop of H.E. Kiewe, British needlepoint-tapestry designer; a display of classical and modern canvases and completed designs of tapestries; and Mrs. Wen-Chi Kwok Hou demonstrating brush-stroke calligraphy. On the sixth floor, there was a replica of a working Big Ben; a "Goldsmith's Hall" exhibition, a rare collection of antique and modern British silver crafted by the Worshipful Company of Goldsmiths from London; the Crown Jewels of England, in replica; David Thomas, a modern British silver and gold jewelry designer; and Raymond Klee, the British painter. The seventh floor featured the Baxters Gourmet Food Shop, a "recreation of a turn-of-the-century grocery shop stocked with present-day Commonwealth delicacies in an atmosphere of traditional charm"; Wedgwood's chess set; plaques and coronation services for Queen Elizabeth; and Royal Doulton's collection of plates made for kings and queens. On the eighth floor there was the World Cup soccer display. The ninth floor featured "Kaleidoscope Orissa," a collection of folk art from India; the "Work of Royal Society of Painters in Water Colours" exhibit; the "Royal Society of Painters-Etchers and Engravers" exhibit and a display by Miss Kitty Kit-Shan Kam and Miss Susan Wai-Ling Chung, Oriental carpet weavers. The citizens of St. Louis could experience art from around the world without boarding a boat or an airplane; all they had to do was visit Famous-Barr.

There were plenty of craft shows and fairs from 1978 to 1981. In 1981, American craft artists were featured as part of the Folklife Festival. Information from Sandy LaRouche gives us a glimpse of the Annual Fair in the City event: "Vendors and craftsmen from the entire country vied for the positions open. The work was juried to include the finest in handcrafted items." There was also entertainment during these events. LaRouche recalls, "One of the performers was the late Howard 'Sandman' Sims, the celebrated tap dancer and Apollo Theater legend."

France was an event theme used often throughout the history of Famous-Barr. In 1965, Sam Clark, the display director, created the window display "A Night at the Paris Opera" to showcase evening formal wear at the downtown store. In 1990, Famous-Barr gave away a trip for two to Paris. The prize included two round-trip airline tickets, accommodations for six nights at the historic France et Choiseul Hotel, a Seine River cruise and a visit to Notre Dame Cathedral.

This French-themed window display by Sam Clark was featured at the Downtown Famous-Barr in 1965. *Courtesy of Missouri History Museum.*

European-themed events made their way through years of promotions at Famous-Barr. Sandy LaRouche, who worked with Helen Weiss in public relations, said, "The British Heritage Festival was one of the major country promotions presented by Famous-Barr." Claudette Franovitch, the secretary of special events, public relations and advertising, modeled a "Berman's

This exterior Viking-style display appeared at the Downtown Famous-Barr for the Scandia exhibition in 1965. *Courtesy of Missouri History Museum.*

and Nathan's costume created for the *Six Wives of Henry VIII*, the BBC production." The costumes were displayed at Downtown Famous-Barr in the ninth-floor auditorium during the British event. Sandy reminisces, "The costumes arrived late and were being held for payment of duty. They billed us in customs as if the paste jewels for the costumes were real. The airport wouldn't release the costumes until somebody paid thousands of dollars. Somebody did straighten it out. We unpacked with very little time to prepare."

Other European events mentioned by Sandy LaRouche were the Three Cheers events. These events featured three countries at a time. One of the events featured Italy, Germany and France; another featured Ireland, Scotland and England. The Scandia event featured the Scandinavian countries of Norway, Denmark and Sweden.

In 1968, the Beautiful American event took place from October 14 to 26. The festivities were kicked off with a parade at the downtown store. The parade started at the front entrance of Famous-Barr and looped

The opening parade was held at the Downtown Famous-Barr for the Beautiful American Festival in 1968. *Courtesy of Missouri History Museum.*

The Tuxedo Marching Band of New Orleans played at the opening parade for Famous-Barr's Beautiful American Festival in 1968. *Courtesy of Missouri History Museum.*

around the block the Famous-Barr building occupied. Leading the parade were two bands brought together by the Smithsonian Institute in Washington, D.C., the Preservation Hall Jazz Band and the Young Tuxedo Marching Brass Band.

In 1980, Carole Jackson wrote the book *Color Me Beautiful* and started the national trend of color analysis. In 1982, there were color analysis events at the Famous-Barr in Clayton and Springfield, Missouri. The advertising stated, "We show the individual how he/she can look younger, thinner, and more attractive by selecting the colors that are harmonious with their skin undertone." It was based on a concept to help customers choose the colors, styles and textures best for their professional looks. "We determine the season (summer, winter, autumn, spring) and advice on what colors are best for the individual and what colors they should avoid." This trend lasted throughout the 1980s. In 1984, Carole Jackson wrote *Color for Men.*

There were plenty of breakfast events at Famous-Barr. One such breakfast was with Famous Bear and St. Louis Cardinals' Fredbird in 1989. The kids,

The Famous Bear and Fredbird mascot for St. Louis Cardinals were present at a Famous-Barr breakfast event in 1989. *Courtesy of Missouri History Museum.*

Famous Bear and Fredbird had breakfast together in the Tea Room on the sixth floor at the Downtown Famous-Barr.

The Famous Bear was born in 1988; Fredbird was born—or hatched—in 1979. Famous Bear plush toys were offered for sale in the stores during the Christmas season. The bears sold for a special price with a merchandise purchase. While the Famous Bear mascot lasted only a few years, Fredbird is still the Cardinals' mascot today. Before Cardinals games, he plays around on the field. Once the game begins, he starts playing with the fans. Fredbird is loved by the fans because he is so much fun, and he plays jokes, dances around and likes to peck fans' heads.

There was always something exciting going on at Famous-Barr. The store promotions and events catered to children, adults, women and men. One of the largest groups it catered to was brides. Brides-to-be shopped in several departments: the bridal shop, housewares, crystal and china, furniture, linens and cosmetics. The bridal fairs at Famous-Barr were held in spring to prepare brides for summer weddings. Until 1989, the bridal fairs had been held at the downtown store. The location was changed to Nortwest Plaza for the spring 1990 bridal fair. Famous-Barr invited local businesses to take part in the fair. It saved brides time and drew large crowds to the store. Karen Dickmann of Dickmann's Boulevard Bakery at 3139 South Grand Avenue participated. Also participating was Pam Meenach from Karen Ann's Cake Decorating. Other bakeries represented were Ms. Helen Lubeley of Lubeley's Bakery at 7815 Watson Road and Mrs. Helen Fletcher at 7467 Kingsbury Boulevard. Mr. Hank Krussel of Hank's Cheescake at 2218 South Big Bend Boulevard also took part. The bakeries provided sheet cakes for serving the attendees and dummy wedding cakes for display. Hank's gave out cheesecake samples while the music of the Arcangelos Strings, two violins and a cello, played in the background.

While the fair attracted more brides than grooms, the gentlemen were not left out; the fair also included a couples cooking school.

Most events targeted either adults or children's audiences, but one event that included people of all ages was the Valentine's Day event. St. Louis artist Joyce Yarborough visited Famous-Barr at Crestwood, Midrivers, Chesterfield and West County to create silhouettes for customers.

There were numerous other events at Famous-Barr, and the ones mentioned are just a few whose records were found in the archives at the Missouri History Museum.

Chapter 8

CUSTOMER APPRECIATION

Eagle Stamps and Customer Contest Prizes

Quadruple Eagle Stamps issued Tuesday only on all cash purchases except alcohol, restaurant, scout and computer department items.
—advertising in the St. Louis Globe-Democrat, *October 18, 1983*

The Eagle Stamp Company was founded in 1903. One of the earliest mentions of Famous-Barr giving out Eagle stamps is in a newspaper article that ran in 1913. The store had a spring exhibit of American and French designs showing the latest styles from ladies' to children's fashions. The story gave a description of the merchandise housed on all four floors with the conclusion, "An added feature Tuesday will be double Eagle stamp day."

On January 31, 1917, there was an article in the *St. Louis Post-Dispatch* listing the owners of the Eagle Stamp Company: David May, Moses Shoenberg, L.D. Shoenberg and I.H. Lesem. Colonel Lesem managed the business. He explained that the stamps worked as a discount for cash purchases. They were also a form of advertising to attract more business. At that time, Eagle Stamp Company was the largest trading stamp company in Missouri. It sold the stamps to merchants at $2.59 per one thousand stamps and then redeemed them at $2.00 per thousand, making a $0.59 markup per one thousand stamps. Profit was made after paying operating expenses and the salaries of forty employees. The profit was then divided among the partners. The company had been in business fourteen years and had not made a profit for the first seven years. Because three of the partners—David May, Moses Shoenberg and L.D. Shoenberg—were the owners of Famous-Barr, many people were

This image is of streetcar number 2276 beginning to round the North Grand Avenue water tower in 1910. *Courtesy of Missouri History Museum.*

under the impression the Eagle Stamp Company was owned by Famous-Barr. It was not; it was a separate company with some of the same owners.

Most of the company's business was in St. Louis, but some of its two thousand accounts were from other areas in Missouri, Illinois and Arkansas. Famous-Barr was its largest account, but they did not get a discount. Famous-Barr paid the same price for the stamps as the smaller businesses. The company had been asked to explain its business practices over concerns that merchants who issued trading stamps sold their merchandise at a higher price than the merchants who did not give out stamps.

Famous-Barr was just one business in St. Louis that gave away Eagle Stamps. In 1912, the Mutoscope Parlor and Theatre, which was located at the northwest corner of Olive Street and Leonard Avenue, gave out stamps to its customers on Tuesdays, Thursdays and Saturdays.

In 1955, with the opening of the Northland store, a memo outlined the Eagle stamp program: "For over 50 years, Eagle Stamps have been awarded to

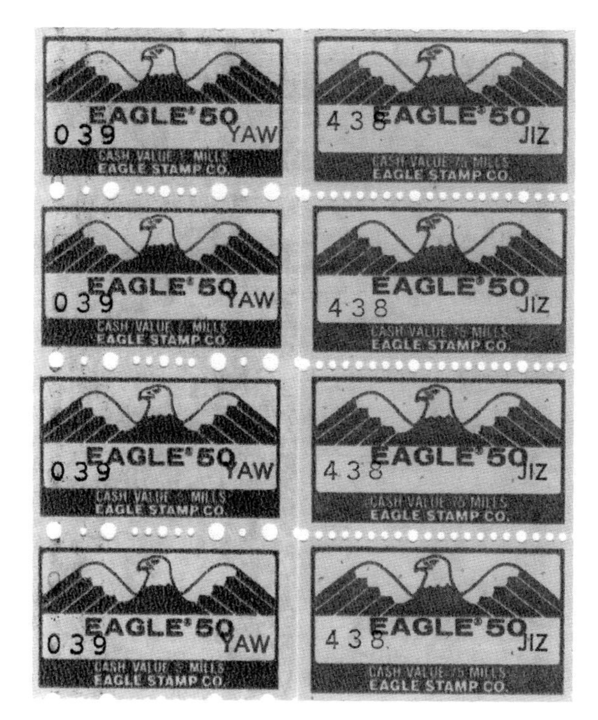

Famous-Barr gave out Eagle Stamps for purchases until 1989 and redeemed them until 1999. *Courtesy of Diane Rademacher.*

Famous-Barr patrons for most purchases of 10 cents or more." The advertising assured customers that stamps would continue to be given out as Famous-Barr added more stores. By 1963, Famous-Barr advertised, "We give and redeem Eagle Stamps: Downtown, Clayton, Southtown and Northland."

In 1964, the Eagle Stamp Company national headquarters moved into new offices in Mill Creek Park at 3100 Market Street. The business moved from the Times Building at 822 North Twelfth Street, where it had occupied three floors. Eagle Stamp claimed to be the largest and oldest stamp firm in St. Louis, employing forty-five office people and serving more than three thousand retailers in Missouri and Illinois.

In an article that ran on June 15, 1976, in the *St. Louis Globe-Democrat*, the Eagle Stamp program was explained to customers. New books filled with 1,500 stamps were worth $3.00 in merchandise or $2.70 in cash. The books that had been issued before June 1976 and were filled with 1,200 stamps had a worth of $2.50 in merchandise and $2.25 cents in cash. The values of the stamps were $0.02 of the sale price of goods and were issued in $0.10, $1.00 and $5.00 denominations. The article went on to say the Eagle Stamp Company had been established in 1903 by the founders of the May Company. Eagle Stamp had been absorbed by the May Department Stores

Company in 1950 and had become a division of the May Department Stores Company in 1962. At this time, it was the third-largest trading stamp company in the United States and the second oldest. Most of the stamps were redeemed for merchandise. You got a better value from merchandise than redeeming the stamps for cash. St. Louis was the only place where stamps could be redeemed for cash.

The stamps were created to serve department stores, but with time, they also served food stores. The largest user of the stamps for food stores was the Cleveland chain Pick N' Pay. In the St. Louis area, the largest outlet for the stamps was National Food Stores, followed by Famous-Barr. Other department stores issuing Eagle Stamps included the May Department Stores Company in Cleveland; Strouss in Youngstown, Ohio; and May-Daniels & Fisher in Denver, Colorado. There were other outlets for the stamps, such as gas and service stations. Some companies gave them out to employees through incentive programs, while other companies issued them for safety awards. Financial institutions gave them out as bonuses for savings and loans and as a way to increase savings and attract new customers. The program was very successful, and more than 90 percent of the stamps issued were redeemed for merchandise or cash.

"We Give and Redeem Eagle Stamps" stated the 1980 St. Louis city directory listing the Famous-Barr stores. The locations listed were: Downtown; Clayton; Southtown; Northland; South County; Northwest; West County; Crestwood; St. Clair, Illinois; and Alton, Illinois.

Eagle Stamps were around for over eighty years. In her book, *Famous Firsts of St. Louis*, Diane Rademacher writes, "The May Company discontinued its Eagle Stamp Division on January 31, 1989, but continued the redemption program for 10 years."

Besides giving out stamps to its customers, Famous-Barr and its vendors gave out lots of prizes in merchandise and trips. The store in Clayton opened in 1948. One of the first events to create excitement for the new opening was a customer contest. Customers were encouraged to enter the contest for a chance to be entertained at the May Department Stores Company New York home headquarters. The first-place winner and their family would be greeted by Victoria the kangaroo. The kangaroo was supplied by Animal Talent Scouts, Incorporated, located at 331 West Eighteenth Street in New York.

In 1963, an ad in the *St. Louis Globe-Democrat* announced "the 29th Children's National Photograph Contest." A first prize would be awarded to one boy and one girl, and each could choose his or her prize from a new Renault R-8 automobile, a Caribbean cruise or a swimming pool. The

Victoria the kangaroo greeted contest winners from St. Louis in New York in 1948. *Courtesy of Missouri History Museum.*

judges for the pictures were Hugh Downs, Henry Fonda, Joanne Woodward, Robert C. Atherton and Maureen O'Hara. Parents were encouraged to have their children's photographs taken in the Famous-Barr Jean Sardou Photo Studios. The stores were offering a half-price contest special, $3.95 for an eight-by-ten portrait, which sold at the regular price of $8.00.

Famous-Barr gave away lots of grand prizes to get shoppers into its stores. Motorized awards were some of the most popular prizes given out in the 1980s. It started out in 1982 with a contest for the promotion the "Successful Woman." Famous-Barr, Revlon and six area Lincoln-Mercury dealers were the sponsors that gave away a royal purple Mercury Scoundrel Limited Edition LN-7.

In 1984, Famous-Barr held its 134th Anniversary Sale. To attract customers into their stores for the sale, Famous-Barr partnered with the Greater St. Louis AMC/Jeep/Renault Advertising Association and encouraged customers to sign up for the grand prize of a brand-new 1984 Renault Encore. The contest brought shoppers into Famous-Barr stores and was good publicity for the AMC/Jeep/Renault Advertising Association.

Winner of a new Plymouth, Paul Tornetto stands between Helen Weiss of Famous-Barr and Ed Sapot of Royal Midtown Chrysler in 1987. *Courtesy of Missouri History Museum.*

In 1987, the motorized prizes continued in the stores and the men's fragrance Drakkar Noir gave away six Yamaha scooters during the Jubilee Sale. Another contest prize for the Jubilee Sale was a 1987 Toyota Corolla FX, sponsored by Jim Lynch Toyota and Famous-Barr. For the Ocean Week promotion, Famous-Barr and Ocean Pacific gave away Yamaha Riva Razz motor scooters to two lucky winners. Another lucky winner in 1987 during the anniversary sale contest was Paul Tornetto, who won a 1987 Plymouth Reliant sponsored by St. Louis Area Chrysler Plymouth dealers.

In 1985, when the Peoria Famous-Barr opened in Illinois, the Grand Opening Sale catalog asked customers to register to win great prizes. One lucky winner would be awarded one million Eagle Stamps, and another two million Eagle Stamps would be awarded to fifty-five customers whose names were drawn from the contest entries. Besides the stamp prizes, over $5,000 of additional prizes would be given away during the contest.

Contests where trips were the grand prizes brought out the crowds, especially for new store openings. In 1990, the Disneyland Trip Giveaway Contest was held for the Northwest Famous-Barr Grand Reopening. The store gave away a round trip for four to Disneyland in Anaheim, California. The contest was sponsored by Famous-Barr, Skyway,

Disneyland, Ramada Inn and Trans World Airlines (TWA) to promote the luggage department.

In August 2001, the West County Grand Reopening Contest gave away many prizes, including a trip. Customers were encouraged to register to win over $35,000 in fabulous prizes throughout the store. One of the prizes was a Disney Land and Sea Trip for four people. It included a four-night stay at Walt Disney World and a four-night cruise.

Famous-Barr could always count on its vendors to help out with prizes, demonstrations and seminars for new store openings and remodel reopenings. In November 1995, for the opening after the remodeling of South County Famous-Barr, the store and its manufacturers gave out some great prizes. Lucky customers had a chance to win prizes from a wide assortment of merchandise, such as a basket of ten women's fragrances valued at $300. Another basket valued at $300 offered customers a choice of products from Elizabeth Arden, Clarins, Monteil, Borghese, Christian Dior or Shiseido. A third basket with a value of $300 was offered with a choice from Estée Lauder, Clinique or Lancome products. Prizes of wardrobes for men valued at $300 each were furnished by Men's Tommy Hilfiger Apparel and the Men's Shoes Department. Prizes of wardrobes for women valued at $300 each were furnished by the following departments: Liz Claiborne, Young Attitudes, Misses Coordinates, Misses, Petites and Womens. A jewelry line provided an eighteen-inch strand of cultured pearls valued at $500. More prizes with a $300 value were awarded in the form of a ladies' shoe wardrobe, Pfaltzgraff dinnerware, a St. John's white goose-down comforter and an intimate apparel wardrobe.

Besides prizes, there were special events for the reopening. Eden Toys provided a person dressed as the character of Peter Rabbit to make a personal appearance. Easy Spirit and Dexter shoes had shoe representatives on hand for fittings. There was informal modeling of the latest trends thoughout the store. The models brought customers into departments where they could meet the experts from Nautica, Polo and Hilfiger. The Napier Jewelry counter was giving away prizes in a spin-to-win contest, and 1928 Jewelry offered engraving. The Housewares Department presented demonstrations by Kitchen Aid, Delonghi, T-Fal, Sunbeam/Oster, Rowenta, Braun, Cuisinart, Krups, Circulon and Calphalon. In the Intimate Apparel Department, the ladies were encouraged to take part in bra-fitting seminars by Bali, Olga and Playtex.

There were so many more events and promotions at Famous-Barr, this selection is a very small sampling of what is in the archives at the Missouri History Museum.

CHAPTER 9

EXPANSION FROM DOWNTOWN

STORES OPEN IN THE COUNTY, ACROSS THE RIVER AND THE REST OF THE STATE

You're never far from Famous-Barr.
—tag line used in advertising starting in 1958

After World War II, business was good for Famous-Barr, and it was time to expand. With the expansion of stores, the company also needed a larger warehouse. The main warehouse and delivery station at Spring Avenue and Market Street opened in the late 1930s and doubled in size in 1947. In 1948, the first Famous-Barr branch store opened in Clayton on Forsyth Boulevard and Jackson Avenue. Stanley Goodman came to St. Louis in 1948. Mr. Goodman took over as the assistant manager for the Clayton Famous-Barr. Later, Stanley Goodman went on to become the president of Famous-Barr, and in 1976, he retired as chairman and chief executive officer of the May Department Stores Company. In 1982, Goodman wrote the book *How to Manage a Turnaround: A Senior Manager's Guide.*

In 1982, the *St. Louis-Globe Democrat* printed an article titled, "Clayton Department Store to Celebrate Its Recent Renovation, Famously Clayton Store." It went on to say that the store had cost $2.75 million to build in 1948, had opened with 111 sales and service departments and covered 208,000 square feet. There had been an estimated five thousand people at the grand opening on October 7, 1948. The 1982 renovation had cost the company $4 million dollars.

This Famous-Barr advertisement is from Polk's St. Louis County Directory of 1957. *Courtesy of Missouri History Museum.*

According to an article in the *St. Louis Post-Dispatch* dated November 1964, architect Noel Leslie Flint designed both the Clayton and Southtown Famous-Barr stores. The article titled "Noel Leslie Flint Dies; Designed Stores Here," announced that Mr. Flint had died in Chicago at the age of

Clayton Famous-Barr at 7425 Forsyth Boulevard is seen here in 1952. *Courtesy of Missouri History Museum.*

Helen Weiss, representing Famous-Barr, accepts a Citation Award from the Clayton commissioners in 1964. *Courtesy of Weiss family.*

sixty. It listed some of his other projects as the Grill Room at the Hotel Pierre in New York City, the Wilshire store in Los Angeles and the Crenshaw and University Hill stores in Denver.

The Clayton store had a special shop called the Bird in Hand, the creation of Evelyn Newman. Mrs. Newman knows retail; she is a family member of the Edison Brothers shoe business. Evelyn had heard about a lady who had opened an antique shop in a department store in Cincinnati and thought the idea might work in St. Louis. She took her suggestion to Stanley Goodman, the president of Famous-Barr, who worked for Morton D. May, the head of the May Department Stores Company. Evelyn says about Goodman, "He had such incredible taste." Goodman asked Evelyn for details about the shop and asked her what she would name the shop. He was not impressed by the answer of the Bird in Hand. Her determination won, however, and Goodman warmed up to the name and got behind the antique shop concept. Evelyn was given a budget for inventory and sent to England to buy the goods. The Bird in Hand opened in 1964, with English antiques and an English taxi. The taxi was bought to deliver customers' purchases from the shop. Of the experience, Evelyn reminisces, "That is what put me in the whole antique-collecting business."

Evelyn Newman remembers the most fun she had at Famous-Barr was when she advertised in *The London Telegraph* that she was looking to buy the entire contents of a castle or manor house. The plan was to bring the items back to St. Louis and house them on the third floor at the Clayton Famous-Barr. After receiving some offers, they did consider one of them. At the end the deal did not go through, but the experience was not wasted. Mrs. Newman informs us, "That really started my interest in antiques."

In 1988, the May Department Stores Company announced Famous-Barr would be moving to the Galleria. The company announced the building of two stores at the Galleria, a Famous-Barr department store and a Lord & Taylor specialty department store. The May Department Stores Company had acquired the Lord & Taylor stores in 1986, when it bought the Associated Dry Goods Corporation.

With a new Famous-Barr store opening at the Galleria in 1991, plans were made to close the Clayton store. The store closing sale for Clayton Famous-Barr started on June 26, 1991. Every item in the store was offered at 35 percent off the regular price. On June 30, all items were at 50 percent off; on July 5, all merchandise was offered at 60 percent off. The final phase of the sale started July 10 at 75 percent off; what was left was sold at 80 percent off so the store would be cleared for the opening of the new Galleria Famous-Barr.

Next, the Southtown Famous-Barr store opened at South Kingshighway and Chippewa in 1951. The plans for this location included customer convenience. The parking lot had an entrance to a tunnel that went from the parking lot to the store so customers did not have to cross the street to enter the store, especially when the weather was bad. This entrance was also the only entrance to be used by employees. Employees had to enter and leave the store using the Tunnelway Entrance in the Block House on the south side of Chippewa Street.

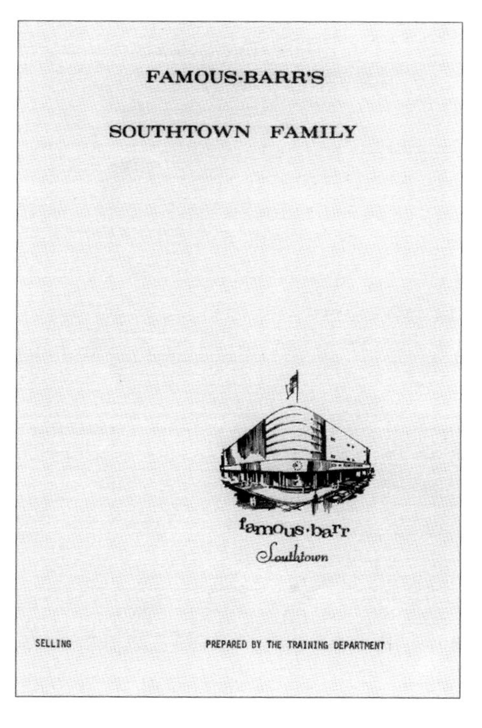

This new employee training manual for Southtown Famous-Barr was given to Gertrude Rademacher circa 1970. *Courtesy of Diane Rademacher.*

The Famous-Barr Southtown training booklet given to Gertrude Rademacher in the early 1970s gives us a hint of the times by listing the customer services offered at the store. Customers had access to baby strollers; a beauty salon; a check room, where customers could check their coats and packages at no charge; a coffee shop; a credit and charge office; an Eagle Stamp redemption desk; gift wrapping; a home furnishings consultant; a hospital where customers and employees could get emergency treatment. Other services offered were hunting and fishing licenses; jewelry repair; and instructions in knitting, crocheting, needlework, hooked rugs and afghans at no charge, but the materials had to be purchased in the store. There was a lost and found department; the Eagle Stamp Desk, which sold merchandise certificates; the Mississippi Room for dining; a department for monogramming; an optical department; a photo studio; a public utility service, which received payments for gas, sewer and electric bills; restrooms; a shoe repair department; a snack bar; public pay phones; a ticket vendor, which sold tickets to Cardinals games, the municipal opera and attractions at the American Theater; and a tire center. The store had four floors: basement, main, second and third.

Salesladies, including Maxine Reitzel, sixth from the left, at Southtown Famous-Barr, circa 1960. *Courtesy of Brenda Sneed and Joyce Chronister.*

The Charga-Plate in the photograph on page 109 was used by Gertrude Rademacher when she shopped at the Southtown Famous-Barr. The first year the Charga-Plate Associates of St. Louis was listed in the city directories was 1937. The business was located at 511 Locust; the president of the company was Kingsley F. Miemoller, and Ercel F. Horner was the treasurer. By 1947, Sig Wolfort was president, W.H. Semsott was secretary and E.F. Horner was treasurer. The business description was listed as processing charge plates. In 1955, Mrs. Anna M. Gillworth was the manager, and the company was still located at 511 Locust. In 1960, the business was still operated by Mrs. Gillworth, but it had moved to 407 Eighth Street, Room 201. The last year

The Charga-Plate was used at Famous-Barr for merchandise charges before store charge cards were issued. *Courtesy of Diane Rademacher.*

Charga-Plate was listed in the St. Louis city directories was in 1971; Louis Delores Sauerwein was the manager.

On October 26, 1991, the *St. Louis Post-Dispatch* article "Famous-Barr to Close Southtown Store" confirmed rumors of the store closing. The article informed us that when Southtown opened in 1951 to a crowd of about one thousand people at the grand opening, there had been 635 salespeople, the store had a bakery and a coffee shop and there had been three parking lots. Now there were only 130 employees and only one parking lot; the other two parking lots had been sold years ago. Southtown Famous-Barr closed in January 1992.

On February 14, 1954, the *St. Louis Post-Dispatch* ran an article titled "Drawing of the Famous-Barr North Side Store." It announced construction was to start immediately; the store would be the first unit in the Northland Shopping Center. The announcement was made by the president of the May Department Stores Company, Morton D. May. It was slated to be the largest Famous-Barr branch store in the St. Louis area.

The Famous-Barr archives unearthed an interesting tidbit of the times from an advertising carriers' company letter to Mr. Leonard Hornbein, director of advertising for Famous-Barr. The letter was dated June 21, 1955. The correspondence stated, "The only Colored population included in our County coverage is largely concentrated in Kinloch and Robertson which is almost 100% Colored. It might be best to put this 3,000 [door-to-door knob hangers announcing the opening of the Northland Famous-Barr store] into St. Charles, Missouri households. I know from experience that these colored people now shop in Wellston and Ferguson. Largely in Wellston because Ferguson Merchants do not cater to them."

The plans for the Northland Famous-Barr store also took a look at transportation to Northland and where customers and employees could get a bite to eat. At this time, bus fares from Baden, Berkeley, Florissant, Highway 66, Ferguson, Dellwood and Jennings to Northland Shopping Center ranged in price from ten to twenty cents. Store plans included three eateries: the Employee's Cafeteria; the Jade Room, a full-fledged restaurant; and the Pick-Quick Room, a snack bar and coffee shop.

In 1955, the Northland store opened at W. Florissant at Lucas Hunt Road. The mailer for the Northland opening advertised, "We give and redeem Eagle Stamps. Naturally you receive Eagle Stamps on almost everything you buy at Famous-Barr Co. This extra savings is a Northland feature, too!" A Northland Famous-Barr pocket guide announced the store would be opening on August 19, 1955. The store would be open on Mondays, Thursdays and Fridays from 9:30 a.m. to 9:30 p.m.; on Tuesdays, Wednesdays and Saturdays, the store would be open from 9:30 a.m. to 5:30 p.m. The store would be closed on Sundays. Customers with charge accounts could use their cards at Famous-Barr Downtown, Clayton, Southtown and Northland. There would be many departments in the store including a Basement Economy Store.

In conversations with former Famous-Barr employees and customers, I found out the Basement Economy Stores had a "One Day Only Dollar Sale" once a month. The crowds were so large during these sales that the fire department had to control the number of people going into the store. The sale was a lot of work for the display department. Every month for one day, the signs for the Dollar Sale went up in the morning and had to come down at the end of the day or before the store opened the next morning.

Morton D. May claimed the new Northland store as "the ultimate in shopping convenience." Judging from the departments listed in the Northland Shopper's Guide, it was indeed a one-stop shop. Mr. May announced that art would also have a place in the store. The newest Famous-Barr store would have murals on the walls painted by Edgar Miller of Chicago and Charles Cobelle of Vermont. These artists had also painted the murals at the Clayton and Southtown stores.

For customer convenience, the Northland Shopper's Guide was printed and given out to shoppers. The guide listed the store's departments by floors.

On the main floor, customers could shop for men's and women's clothing, shoes and accessories, which included gloves, handkerchiefs, hosiery and hats. The bakery and candy counter were also on the main floor. Other departments located on this floor that are not found in today's department stores included: the Book Shop, Religious Goods, Cameras, Typewriters, Flowers, Notions, the Smoke Shop, Sporting Goods, Stationery, Toiletries and Drugs.

The second floor housed departments selling apparel for the entire family. But most of the departments on this floor sold things no longer available in department stores. These departments included Art Needlework, Boy Scout and Girl Scout Shops, Corsets, Decorative Flowers, Uniforms, Fur Salon, Jewelry Repair, Millinery, Nursery Furniture, Patterns, Sewing Machines and Yard Goods.

On the third floor, customers could purchase appliances, dinette sets, housewares, household cleaning supplies, furniture and bedding. Other departments on this floor popular in 1950s department stores included Fireplace Fixtures, Floor Coverings, Ready to Paint Furniture, Hardware, Paints, Records, Phonograph, Television and Radio. Customers could also pay their utility bills on this floor.

The Basement Economy Store was a store within a store selling clothes, furniture and household items. The exhibition hall and garden center (in season) were on this basement floor.

Famous-Barr was a fashion leader, and the Northland store reflected this in the 1950s. Wanda Jennings, a former model and Mrs. America of 1955 was the fashion coordinator at Northland. She directed the models in the Jade Room, where stylish young ladies walked around showing off the latest fashions while customers dined. Models were needed for the many fashion programs offered at the store, and Jennings was in charge of these models. Mrs. Jennings had qualified for the job by being selected America's outstanding housewife in a weeklong competition. Mrs. Jennings, along with her family, and all the other state finalists and their families had to live in model homes during the week of the contest. The women were judged on their sense of style and homemaking skills. The competition included house

The Bridal Department at Downtown Famous-Barr in 1960. *Courtesy of Missouri History Museum.*

cleaning, ironing, sewing and the ability to plan and prepare meals. The message was, "You can be a homemaker and a stylish fashion figure too!"

In 1980, the Northland store celebrated its twenty-fifth anniversary. There were demonstrations in cooking, microwave uses and applying makeup. There were also fashion shows and a Barbie Doll event. The featured event was a special guest appearance by Darth Vader from *Star Wars* and *The Empire Strikes Back*.

Every Famous-Barr store had a bridal salon, including Northland. The Bridal Departments at Famous-Barr created so many special family memories. The expert salesladies and seamstresses took the time to listen to the brides and their wedding party to make sure the wedding attire was perfect on their special day. For years, the store downtown held a bridal fair to help brides and grooms prepare for their big day. An example of this was in 1987, when brides and grooms-to-be were invited to a party. The party was to take place on Saturday and Sunday and begin in the ninth-floor auditorium. The topic for the event was "A World of Ideas."

The guests would learn how to plan their weddings and how to select the right merchandise for their homes. There were also seminars for the brides-to-be on hair and makeup. For the soon-to-be couples, there were product demonstrations on the seventh floor in the Market Place in the Housewares Department. These demos would give the couples ideas of what they might need in their kitchens. To make the event more fun there were prizes and drawings. The prizes included the usual flatware, china, table linens, towels, lingerie, cookware and small appliances. For the brides, there was a prize of a dozen pairs of Calvin Klein hosiery and an eighteen-inch Add-A-Bead Starter Necklace.

Former brides who had shopped at the Northland Famous-Barr and heard of the Downtown Bridal Fairs from the salesladies would be shopping in a different store in 1993. On April 14, 1992, an article in the *St. Louis Post-Dispatch* titled "Famous Store for Jamestown, But Store Will Close at Northland Center" announced the closing of Northland Famous-Barr. In 1993, the Northland store closed, and the Jamestown store opened.

South County Famous-Barr opened August 2, 1963, in the South County Shopping Center. It opened to the fanfare of Famous-Barr's "Store of the Future," and this store would be the first of the store buildings to be designed with a dome. It was the company's fourth suburban store in the St. Louis area. The building was designed by Raymond Loewy and William Snaith Inc., with Strobel and Rongved as consulting engineers. The focal point of the structure was a sculptured rotunda or central cupola dome. South County Famous-Barr was the first store to feature the unusual exterior dome with the interior rotunda, which was a striking architectural design element of the new building. Associate architects were Hellmuth, Obata and Kassabaum. The general contractor was Buckley Construction Company. The shopping center was designed as the latest innovation in a retail facility: the enclosed shopping mall. In 1963, there were only three air-conditioned malls in St. Louis County: Town and Country Mall, River Roads Shopping Center and South County Shopping Center. The store hours in 1963 were 9:30 a.m. to 9:30 p.m., Mondays through Saturdays.

In 1995, the South County store went through a major remodeling. Advertising for the Famous-Barr South County Grand Reopening encouraged customers to "see the difference! Join us for exciting events & great prizes."

Northwest Plaza Famous-Barr opened in St. Ann in 1966. The building also featured the sculptured rotunda design. Business at this store and the

other Famous-Barr locations went along as usual, until the 1980s. The 1980s brought about changes at Famous-Barr, one of which would be closing the chapter on selling toys. An article that ran in the *St. Louis Post-Dispatch* on April 1, 1985, announced that Famous-Barr would be phasing out toy departments. The toy departments in South County, Belleville, Downtown, Northwest Plaza and North County stores were going to be discontinued. For the last two years, Famous-Barr had been leasing its toy departments to Kay Bee Toys, and it was time to convert the selling space to more profitable product lines.

Famous-Barr kept expanding, and its original goal from the early 1900s—"To provide all things to all people"—was still very much in place in the 1960s. Evidence of this business model was found in an article in the *St. Louis Globe-Democrat* dated May 27, 1967. The title read "Famous-Barr to Offer Car Rental Service." The piece started out, "Starting Thursday, Famous-Barr Company will become the first department stores in the United States to offer its customer a car rental service." The service was offered at Northland, Clayton, South County and Northwest Plaza Famous-Barr stores. The rental models included prestige, economy and sports cars. The rental costs started at six dollars a day and six cents per mile, and the costs were based on twenty-four-hour days and the minimum rental was one day. For four dollars and six cents a mile, you could rent a car overnight. The overnight hours were from 5:30 p.m. until 10:30 a.m. Customers could charge their car rentals to their Famous-Barr credit cards and receive Eagle Stamps for their rentals. The Famous-Barr Rent-a-Car rentals were to be picked up at the stores' parking lots.

Crestwood Famous-Barr opened in St. Louis County in September 1969 in the Crestwood Plaza Shopping Center. The store opened with a 150-seat Tea Room offering both a lunch and dinner menu. In addition, there was another smaller area serving sandwiches and the Famous French Onion Soup. The opening ceremonies on September 15 started out with an invitation-only champagne breakfast, followed by a Red Carpet Opening Ceremony, which was open to the public. The Crestwood store was the

Opposite, top: The grand opening of the South County Famous-Barr drew crowds of shoppers in 1963. *Courtesy of Missouri History Museum.*

Opposite, bottom: The Northwest Plaza Famous-Barr opened in 1966, and this image was taken in 1969. *Courtesy of Missouri History Museum.*

eighth Famous-Barr store to open in the St. Louis area. The press release read, "This store is the ultimate in the shop concept; The Store within a Store, and is dedicated to fashion for the entire family and for the home." At this time, Sanford J. Zimmerman was the president of Famous-Barr. Fashion designer Anne Klein was the special guest for the opening event.

West County Famous-Barr originally opened in 1969 in Des Peres at the West County Center. In 2001, the new West County store opened with a grand-opening celebration and ribbon-cutting ceremony on August 15. There were the usual retail events of informal modeling, trunk shows, fashion shows and cosmetic makeovers.

In the Children's Department, the opening event was something different from other store openings prior to 2001. There was a Barbie Look-A-Like Event, and kids who took their picture with Barbie in the Children's Department would be given a special gift to take home. Another event in the Children's Department was a book signing by Dan Martin. He was promoting his book, *The Story of the First 100 Years of the St. Louis Post-Dispatch Weatherbird*.

In the Housewares Department, there were cooking demonstrations by local chefs, including Matt McGuire of King Louie's, caterer Bryan Young, Rich Lo Russo of Lo Russo's Cucina and David Timney of Balaban's. Cooking classes were offered with Chef Doug Knopp of Clark Street Grill.

There was a karaoke contest hosted by 93.7 DJ Craig Cornett, and five lucky winners received a free karaoke machine. Sprint PCS invited customers to meet professional bowler Orlando Pace, who greeted guests and signed autographs. Fans also came by to meet Hall of Fame baseball legend Lou Brock, who had played for the St. Louis Cardinals.

The first Famous-Barr to open in Illinois was at St. Clair Square in Fairview Heights. The store opened in October 1973 and held reopening celebrations in 1983.

The Plaza Frontenac Famous-Barr opened in 1974, operating under the name FB, Ltd. An article titled "Famous-Barr Frontenac Store Closing" in the *St. Louis Post-Dispatch* on October 3, 1987, gives us an idea of the concept behind this store. The article stated this was the only store of the eighteen Famous-Barr stores to sell only women's fashions. The store had opened twelve years ago, occupying two floors adding up to thirty-two thousand square feet. Eula Fulton, buyer of designer clothes for Famous-Barr, stocked the store and import shop with the latest trends in ladies' fashions. Two designer sportswear labels featured at FB, Ltd., were Gene Ewing and Finity. The Frontenac store closed in 1987.

The second Famous-Barr store to open in Illinois and the first store located out of the St. Louis home market was in Springfield. The store opened at White Oaks Mall in August 1977. Springfield, Illinois, is located about one hundred miles north of St. Louis. For the grand opening, Charlotte Ford made a personal appearance in the Designer Sportswear Department.

Alton Famous-Barr opened in Alton Square in Illinois in 1978. It was the twelfth Famous-Barr and the third store in Illinois. The Junior League of Greater Alton teamed up with Famous-Barr for a pre-opening benefit gala on October 13, 1978. Ten thousand invitations were mailed out, and 1,500 tickets for the preview cocktail party were sold at ten dollars per person. The celebrity guest at the gala was Beverly Sassoon, former Columbia Pictures actress and the spokeswoman for Vidal Sassoon, Incorporated. Beverly, the wife of Vidal Sassoon, co-wrote the book *A Year of Beauty and Health*. All the money raised went to the Junior League to help finance its community programs. Also entertaining at the gala were dancing sensations Lynn Dyvig and David Schnitze, who demonstrated the latest disco steps in the Junior Department.

The Alton Famous-Barr officially opened October 16, 1978. On October 19, fashion designer Bill Blass made an appearance as part of the store's

A highlight of the 1978 grand opening of the Alton Famous-Barr was a fashion show staged under a disco ball, a fixture of the discotheques in the 1970s. *Courtesy of Missouri History Museum.*

grand opening. At this time, Bill Blass's name was on more than fifty products. For the store opening, he was promoting his Bill Blass perfume and brought along models dressed in his designs. The models walked around the store giving out free samples of Bill Blass perfume, which sold at $100 an ounce.

The thirteenth Famous-Barr store opened in 1981 in Cape Girardeau, Missouri, in the West Park Mall. The project architects were Kenneth Balk and Associates from St. Louis. The design architects were Amato-Reed Associates, also of St. Louis. The grand opening was on March 5.

When it opened, the store declared itself "the largest department store company serving the St. Louis, Missouri and Springfield, Illinois markets." A newspaper article on February 26, 1981, in the *Southeast Missourian* announced that Walter S. Hosea, a ninety-year-old Cape Girardeau resident and the father of Walter Hosea, would be cutting the ribbon at the grand opening. Walter Hosea was the vice-president in charge of Famous-Barr branch store operations.

One of the features of the store was the candy department. The candy was made in St. Louis in the Famous-Barr candy kitchen and shipped to Cape Girardeau. Another store highlight was the Famous French Onion Soup available at the Golden Eagle II Restaurant.

To encourage people to come out to see the new store, there were customer drawings for prizes. The main drawing was for a 1981 Chevette Scooter presented by Coad Chevrolet. Another drawing was for 100,000 Eagle Stamps, one winner of 50,000 stamps and two winners of 25,000 stamps each. Other prizes during the grand opening included a Zenith portable color television set and an eighteen-inch, fourteen-karat gold chain. The kids could have their picture taken with the fuzzy Garanimal characters. Garanimals was a brand of children's clothing with Dr. Joyce Brothers as spokesperson for the company.

In 1981, the Midrivers Mall project was stalled, but the Midrivers Famous-Barr opened on August 3, 1981. The business opened as a free-standing store with the restaurant Pappa Fabarre. The store opened with two levels covering 164,000 square feet. The building was designed by Amato-Reed Associates of St. Louis, with additional architectural assistance by Kenneth Balk and Associates.

Midrivers Mall was not constructed until 1985. The *St. Louis Post-Dispatch* ran an article on April 11, 1985, giving readers the details. Midrivers Famous-Barr had opened before Midrivers Mall because the company building the mall, May Stores Shopping Center, Inc., couldn't secure two additional major stores for the mall project in 1981. In 1985, the mall opened, and in

Magician Jeff Lefton entertained the children at the grand opening of Midrivers Famous-Barr in 1981. *Courtesy of Missouri History Museum.*

1997, Famous-Barr expanded its store. In July 2000, after remodeling the store, Midrivers Famous-Barr had a reopening celebration.

Springfield Famous-Barr opened at Battlefield Mall in Springfield, Missouri, on November 6, 1982. It was the fifteenth Famous-Barr store. To celebrate, customers were encouraged to register to "be an Eagle Stamp Millionaire!" One lucky customer would be the winner of one million Eagle Stamps. Another two million Eagle Stamps were given out to a total of fifty-six winners. In 1982, Eagle Stamps redeemed at Famous-Barr were valued as follows; filled books were worth $4.00 in merchandise or $3.60 in cash. Customers got one "10" stamp with each $1.00 purchased; "50" stamps were also given out for the equivalent of five "10" stamps. Tuesdays were double Eagle Stamp day. The advertising for the grand opening reminded Famous-Barr customers that it had been giving away Eagle Stamps for almost eighty years and this was the store's way of saying thank you to its loyal customers.

Besides stamps, the store also gave out over $12,000 in prizes during the grand opening. In 1998, the store was expanded and remodeled.

At the 1983 grand opening for the Chesterfield Famous-Barr, crowds waited patiently for the doors to open so they could get a glimpse of the new store. *Courtesy of Missouri History Museum.*

The original Chesterfield Famous-Barr opened August 3, 1983. In 1995, the Chesterfield store got a new look: a new three-level store. A store flier filled with coupons for November 1 through November 5, 1995, encouraged customers to come to the Chesterfield store to take a look and register to win "Fabulous Prizes." These prizes included an Estée Lauder basket, a Chanel women's/men's basket, a Dooney & Bourke handbag and leather accessory wardrobe, a ladies' shoe wardrobe, a men's Polo wardrobe and a men's tailored clothing wardrobe. Each of these prizes was valued at $1,000. There were other prizes for women, including a basket of Borghese, Prescriptives or Shiseido products; a combination basket of Lancôme, Christian Dior or Clarins products; a basket of Elizabeth Arden or Monteil products; a Clinique basket; and fifteen different baskets of women's fragrances. These prizes were all valued at $300 each. Other prizes with a $300 value were ten different baskets of men's fragrances, a Polo/Ralph Lauren handbag, a fashion watch collection, a young men's Levi's wardrobe, a men's Levi's Dockers wardrobe, a men's activewear wardrobe, a Tommy Hilfiger wardrobe, a men's Liz Claiborne wardrobe, a men's Guess wardrobe, a men's Nautica wardrobe and men's Haggar suit separates. There was one prize valued

The new Famous-Barr store in Peoria, Illinois, opened in 1985. *Courtesy of Missouri History Museum.*

at $400, a fourteen-karat gold necklace, and one valued at $500, an eighteen-inch strand of cultured pearls.

The *Peoria Journal Star* ran an article announcing the opening of Famous-Barr's seventeenth store at Northwoods Mall in Peoria, Illinois. The article, titled "Famous-Barr Given Royal Treatment at Opening," was printed on October 3, 1985. On October 2, there had been a concert at the store to benefit the Peoria Symphony Orchestra. The concert had attracted about six hundred people. The next day, the store opened with a base staff of 350 employees. The grand opening had included clowns, a high school band and singing. The article mentioned that this Famous-Barr store building did not have enough room for a restaurant.

On February 22, 1987, the *Joplin Globe* publicized the opening of Famous-Barr in Northpark Mall in Joplin, Missouri. The store opened on March 5, 1987, and that day the *St. Louis Post-Dispatch* printed an article giving details about the latest Famous-Barr store. The store opened with 175 employees. The eighty-five-thousand-square-foot, single-level store was designed by Kenneth Balk and Associates of St. Louis. Famous-Barr was one of the anchor stores for the mall, along with Venture, also owned by the May Department Stores Company. One of the grand-opening events that created the most excitement was the imprinting of children's hands in wet cement outside the store. Children selected were kids who had birthdays in March. In 1995, the store went through a remodeling and had a reopening celebration in September.

In 1986, L.S. Ayers & Company in the state of Indiana was added to the May Department Stores Company. The L.S. Ayers stores included

The L.S. Ayers and Company clock in downtown Indianapolis was designed in 1936. *Courtesy of Missouri History Museum.*

Downtown, Lafayette Square, Castleton, Glendale and Washington Square in Indianapolis; Southtown and Glenbrook in Fort Wayne; Scottsdale and University Park in South Bend; Lafayette; Bloomington; Muncie; Greenwood; Merrillville and Evansville.

In 1996, the May Department Stores Company announced, "The opening of our Famous-Barr store at Eastland Mall in Evansville will mark our entry into the southern Indiana market." The Evansville store was the only store in Indiana to be named Famous-Barr. All the other Indiana stores retained the L.S. Ayres name.

The L.S. Ayres & Company clock was designed by Arthur Bohn of Vonnegut, Bohn & Mueller in 1936. It was mounted at the corner of the Downtown Indianapolis L.S. Ayres store at Meridian and Washington Streets. The clock weighs six thousand pounds, and the supporting brackets weigh another four thousand pounds. The clock was restored in 1978.

In 1972, L.S. Ayers celebrated its 100th anniversary; the company had started out as N.R. Smith and Ayres. In 1874, Lyman Ayres took over the business, and the name was changed to L.S. Ayres & Company.

CHAPTER 10

A LANDMARK DISAPPEARS

FAMOUS-BARR IS NOW MACY'S

The only thing constant in life is change.
—Francois de la Rochefoucauld

Famous-Barr survived economic and labor changes for almost a century. Business carried on through World Wars I and II, the aftermath of the 1929 Stock Market Crash, the Great Depression in the 1930s, the civil rights movement in the 1960s and the repealing of the Missouri blue law. Each decade had presented its challenges, but the company had persevered.

Now as we look back, it would be easy to say Famous-Barr was just a corporation with no emotions, but after going through the records, the archives and talking to former employees and customers, it is evident that Famous-Barr touched the lives of so many people.

During World War II, there was only one Famous-Barr, the store downtown. The employees were a close-knit group and enjoyed hearing how their work colleagues were doing in the military. In the May 5, 1944 *Store Chat* issue, there was a page dedicated to Famous-Barr employees in the service. The page was titled "The Famous Legion: More Letters from Our Boys and Girls in the Service." The men and women who worked at Famous-Barr and were now in the service wrote letters to employees at the store to be published in *Store Chat*.

Private Jewell Coleman worked in housewares on the seventh floor and was stationed in Atlanta, Georgia. Coleman wrote, "I think the Famous Pin-Up Girl idea is wonderful, as do the rest of my company." On the back cover

Store Chat was published for Famous-Barr employees. During World War II, a copy went out to all Famous-Barr employees who were serving in the military. *Courtesy of Missouri History Museum.*

of this 1944 issue, the pinup girl was Melba Pauly. Miss Pauly was a blue-eyed American beauty, and she was five feet, five inches tall. The servicemen were encouraged to put Miss Pauly on their walls "and just try to forget!"

A note followed about Private Norman Winkler, mentioning he had come by the store to see his fellow Famousites after basic training in Fort Benning, Georgia. In another note, Major Charles Taylor had left for the service in 1940 and came by the store in 1944 to see his former associates. The note ended, "Good luck, Major Taylor! Along with America, the Famous Family salutes you." One entry mentioned that Private Ed Meeker had been home in St. Louis on a ten-day furlough from Camp Roberts, California. He was hoping to return to his job in the Basement Shoe Department soon. Another entry was about Marie Richardson from Basement Balcony Domestics, who had come by to say hello on her way to an appointment at the Red Cross Blood Bank. Her service job was at the WAC headquarters keeping records. The entry went on to say that one of her sons was on furlough with Marie, while her other son was in New Guinea. There was a note about a banquet for Corporal Bill Burke from the Advertising Department. The art director for Famous-Barr, Norrie Passino, had made a luncheon date with Bill and then surprised him with sixteen of his friends from advertising.

More news followed. Private Francis X. Picarelli from the Furniture Department wrote a letter to Mr. Buckland. He wanted to let Buckland know he was getting ready to start his third week of basic training at S. Camp Hood, Infantry Replacement Training Center, in Texas. He wrote, "It seems like I have been gone from the store for years, and I certainly hope my return is not too far in the future." The last entry was about Private Werner Born, who had visited the store, where he was greeted with a big welcome sign in the Men's Furnishing Department. He was on his way from Camp Fannin, Texas, to Fort Ord in California.

Famous-Barr appreciated its employees serving their country and wanted to make sure the service people knew it. A copy of *Store Chat* was mailed to each one of the employees serving in the military.

Ethel Foster and other black elevator operators were hired at Famous-Barr downtown in the 1940s at a time when many businesses did not employ African Americans. In 1947, when Ethel was hired, the color of her skin helped get her foot in the door of the place where she would work for the next thirty-eight years. Because Ethel was a light-skinned black woman, she had opportunities dark-skinned blacks did not have at this time in America.

Researching the 1947 help-wanted ads gives us a glimpse of what it was like to be a black woman looking for a job in St. Louis. An ad that ran

The ladies in the white-collar dresses were elevator operators at the Downtown Famous-Barr in the late 1940s; Ethel Foster is in the center of the first row. *Courtesy of Missouri History Museum.*

in the *St. Louis Post-Dispatch* on June 1, 1947, read: "Help Wanted, Woman Elevator Operator, white, 40 hour week; experience not necessary, Room 302 Missouri Theater Bldg." Another ad on June 2, 1947, read: "Help Wanted, Woman Elevator Operators, white, size 12–14 uniform, apply Miss Finney, Mark Twain Hotel." On the same date, another ad read: "Help Wanted, Woman Elevator Operator, colored, small, neat, experience not necessary, 4402 McPherson, Hampton Hall Apts." This is what the times were like when Ethel Foster applied for a job as an elevator operator and got hired at Famous-Barr.

While doing the research for this book, I found another lady who had worked at Famous-Barr as an elevator operator. Her name was Estella Howard, and her daughter Angela Howard remarked that her mother was eighteen or nineteen when she was hired at the Famous-Barr downtown store. Estella, like Ethel Foster, was a light-skinned black woman, and she worked at Famous from 1958 to 1961.

Mrs. Foster saw many changes in St. Louis and at Famous-Barr; one of the most important was the change in hiring practices. Another was the repealing of the Missouri blue law in 1983. The blue law kept retail stores closed on Sundays. The *St. Louis Globe-Democrat* made the announcement on October 20, 1983. The article, "Sunday Sales to Become Reality This Weekend," invited customers to shop on Sunday in downtown St. Louis. St. Louis mayor Vincent Schoemehl was the first Sunday customer at the Downtown Famous-Barr. The mayor was greeted by Famous-Barr president and CEO, Richard L. Battram.

Famous-Barr and Stix, Baer & Fuller paid their employees overtime to work a seven-hour shift on Sundays from 11:00 a.m. to 6:00 p.m. Employees got paid time and a half to work Sundays. The new law authorizing retail sales on Sundays had become legal in downtown St. Louis on October 5, 1983.

The Sunday retail store openings led the way for stores to open on holidays. A Famous-Barr ad in the *St. Louis Post-Dispatch* that ran on December 31, 1985, declared, "First time ever: open New Year's Day!" The advertising encouraged customers to shop from 10:00 a.m. to 6:00 p.m. Later, malls and shopping centers would be open on all holidays except Thanksgiving and Christmas.

Ethel Foster started out as an elevator operator and later was promoted to the Cosmetics Department at the Downtown Famous-Barr. Ethel is shown here in the late 1950s. *Courtesy of Missouri History Museum.*

Ethel Foster worked for the May Department Stores Company for thirty-eight years before she retired in 1985. Her entire career was as an employee at the downtown store. After working as an elevator operator for a few years, she was promoted to the Cosmetics Department, making twenty-one dollars a week.

Mrs. Foster always carried herself in a professional manner; she had gone to college and had great people skills. Her traits were noticed by Mr. May, who gave her a desk and a phone and invited her to represent blacks at Famous-Barr events. After working in cosmetics, Ethel worked herself up to the Credit Department. There she helped customers fill out credit applications, and she collected on past-due accounts.

When Ethel first went to work for the May Department Stores Company, not all employees were allowed to buy company stocks through profit-sharing plans. As soon as they were permitted to take part in profit sharing, Ethel took the opportunity to participate and was able to take advantage of her plan when she retired. Even though she suffered through the inequalities of being black and a woman, she informs us that she has had a good life. She says, "I have lived to ninety years. I have done something right, for God has given me a good life. I will always treat my brothers and sisters as lost friends." Her advice for a good life is: "Do right, have a good heart, treat people well and be who you are."

At the time this book goes to print, Miss Ethel is ninety-one. She is still very active as a member of Mount Olive Baptist Church and is the last original surviving member of the Legend Singers of St. Louis. The Legend Singers were founded in 1940.

When Famous-Barr was established in 1911, the ladies were driven downtown in horse-driven carriages or took streetcars to the store. Then the automobile came into use, and in 1922, Famous-Barr built a two-level garage that held four hundred cars. It was near the store on Seventh Street. By the early 1960s, the old garage was too small and outdated. Business was still good downtown. People enjoyed going into the city to shop, dine and be entertained. In 1962, it was time to build a new larger garage. This time, the garage would be attached to Famous-Barr and more convenient for customers. The garage featured a skyway to get from the garage into the store and headquarter offices.

Famous-Barr was proud of the new garage and took every opportunity to use the construction site as a reminder to St. Louis that Famous-Barr was keeping up with the times. When construction was complete, there were plenty of May Department Stores Company and Famous-Barr executives,

Model posing at construction site for the new Downtown Famous-Barr parking garage, 1962. *Courtesy of Missouri History Museum.*

along with members of the press, to witness the cutting of the ribbon for the official opening.

As the business of Famous-Barr had continued to grow and more stores were opened, marking and receiving needed a larger space. The original

May Department Stores Company executives and members of the media gather at the Downtown Famous-Barr parking garage grand opening in 1962. President Stanley Goodman is in the light-colored suit and dark tie in the front row. *Courtesy of Missouri History Museum.*

warehouse, which had been built around 1900 and had been used by Famous-Barr for almost twenty-five years, would be abandoned and demolished in 1938. The old warehouse had five stories and was downtown at the southwest corner of Broadway and Franklin. The new warehouse was built at Spring and Vandeventer. In the 1970s, the Famous-Barr warehouse was located at 3728 Market Street. In the 1976–77 phone directory, the warehouse was listed at 3728 Market Street, and the fixture (display and racks) warehouse was listed at 3800 Market Street. The Famous-Barr Warehouse Store was listed at 3700 Market.

Businesses, like people, are not born old; there is a life that has been lived from birth to death. It's what happens between those two points that sums up a life well lived, and Famous-Barr, along with the May Department Stores Company, lived a very good life. As the May Department Stores Company grew, it was hard to imagine it all got started with one store in Leadville,

The Famous-Barr warehouse was located at 3728 Market Street in 1978. *Courtesy of Missouri History Museum.*

In 1978, the Famous-Barr Warehouse Store was located next to the warehouse at 3700 Market Street, 1978. *Courtesy of Missouri History Museum.*

Colorado, in the 1870s. By 2006, May Department Stores Company was one of the largest retailers in America. That position was accomplished by the May Department Stores Company acquiring companies all over the United States.

The Railway Exchange Building was home to the Downtown Famous-Barr department store and the headquarters of the May Department Stores Company; this photograph was taken in 1967. *Courtesy of Missouri History Museum.*

According to an article in the *St. Louis Globe Democrat* dated April 29, 1969, the May Department Stores Company, based in St. Louis, operated eighty-four stores. At this time, Stanley Goodman was the president of the May Company. Goodman had been president of Famous-Barr from 1959 to 1967. In 1967, he was named president of the May Department Stores Company. He would keep that post until 1976. The Goodman period was one of great growth for the company.

In 1976, May Department Stores Company operated 129 department and discount stores and 58 catalog showroom stores. The catalog showrooms had opened in 1973 in New York and San Francisco. By 1977, there were 68 showrooms with 4 new ones scheduled to open that year. The Venture Discount Stores division owned by May Department Stores Company had opened its first store in 1970 and was doing business in three states. In 1976, it opened 2 stores in Missouri: Maplewood and in the Festus–Crystal City area. At this time, the Venture stores included 9 stores in the St. Louis area; 6 in the Kansas City area; 3 stores in Chicago; 1 store in Springfield, Missouri; and 1 in Peoria, Illinois. Famous-Barr had 10 stores in the St. Louis area.

In 1977, the May Department Stores Company advertised entering its 100th year of business. It was a long way from the first store founded in the mining camp in Leadville, Colorado, and it was a business David May could not have imagined when he moved the May Company headquarters to St. Louis in 1905. By 1977, the company he founded had grown to owning eleven department store companies, which included May Department Stores Company, Los Angles; the Hecht Company, Washington-Baltimore; Famous-Barr, St. Louis; Kaufmann's, Pittsburgh; May Department Stores Company, Cleveland; Meier & Frank, Oregon; G. Fox & Company, Hartford; M. O'Neil, Akron; May D & F, Denver; Strouss, Youngston; and May-Cohens, Jacksonville. The May Department Stores Company operated a total of 113 stores.

The May Department Stores Company continued to grow and had a strong presence in St. Louis. By 1985, the May Department Stores Company owned Famous-Barr and forty-eight Payless Shoe Source stores in the St. Louis area.

The May Department Stores Company kept buying out more companies, and in 1990, it was one of the largest retailers in the United States. The company operated 290 department stores; 2,704 specialty shoe stores; and 75 Venture stores. It operated department stores in fourteen states, which included Lord & Taylor, New York; Foley's, Houston; May Department Stores Company, California; Hecht's, Washington, D.C.; Robinson's, Los

Angeles; Kaufmann's, Pittsburgh; Famous-Barr, St. Louis; Filene's, Boston; May Department Stores Company, Ohio; G. Fox, Hartford, Connecticut; L.S. Ayres, Indianapolis; May D&F, Denver; Meier & Frank, Portland, Oregon; and Sibley's, Rochester, New York. It also operated Venture stores in eight states, and Volume Shoe operated in forty-three states.

The business kept changing, and in 1996, the May Department Stores Company moved 400 jobs to its credit collection office in Earth City, Missouri. Fifty employees came from Maryland after the closing of the credit collection office for its Hecht's chain. The other 350 jobs were filled locally. The credit department in Earth City worked on collections for Famous-Barr and Lord & Taylor. That same year, Famous-Barr in St. Louis had over $1 billion in sales and operated 30 department stores in Missouri, Illinois and Indiana under the names of Famous-Barr and L.S. Ayers.

Business continued to be good, and in 1997, Famous-Barr operated thirty stores and employed 9,500 people in Missouri, Illinois and Indiana under Famous-Barr and L. S. Ayres. In the same year, May Company operated 366 stores in thirty states and the District of Columbia. The May Department Stores Company located at 611 Olive Street in St. Louis included Famous-Barr, St. Louis; Lord & Taylor, New York; Strawbridge's, Philadelphia; Hecht's, Washington, D.C.; Foley's, Houston; Robinson's-May, Los Angeles; Filene's, Boston; L.S. Ayres, Indianapolis; Kaufmann's, Pittsburgh; and Meier & Frank in Portland, Oregon.

By 2001, May Department Stores Company had added the Jones Store, Kansas City; ZCMI, Salt Lake City; and David's Bridal, Philadelphia. In 2003, the company added After Hours Formalwear, Atlanta; and Priscilla of Boston, and it no longer owned ZCMI. At this time, May Department Stores Company was operating 445 department stores in forty-five states, including the District of Columbia and Puerto Rico.

The company that had been acquiring other companies for decades was now the one being bought out by Macy's, the largest department store company in the United States. An August 20, 2006 article in the *St. Louis Business Journal* written by Christopher Tritto announced the demise of Famous-Barr. The title read, "Famous-Barr Checks Out as Macy's Makes Its Debut." The article stated that in three weeks, the Famous-Barr banner would come down, the Macy's signs would go up and, on September 9, more than four hundred May Department Stores across the United States would officially relaunch as Federated Department Stores.

While Federated Department Stores' stock price went up, so did the sentiments over Famous-Barr. St. Louisans took offense to the remarks made about Macy's stepping up the quality and style of the clothing and other lines carried by the St. Louis department store Famous-Barr. Emotions ran deep; this is where so many of St. Louis' citizens created lifetime memories. This was the place where their great-grandparents, grandparents and they themselves shopped for their weddings, proms and so many other special occasions. Famous-Barr in downtown St. Louis had marked the beginning of the Christmas holiday season for so many generations, and this tradition was coming to an end.

Macy's rolled in with its private labels, including INC, Alfani, Tasso Elba, Charter Club and other labels that had brought them success in other markets. The only Famous-Barr private labels would now be found in coats and hats in local vintage and thrift stores.

Macy's also planned to widen the aisles in the stores so the departments would not be as cluttered as before. One of the positive changes was the installation of scanners throughout the store where customers could check prices on their own, instead of having to ask a salesperson behind the counter. There was also a three-year plan to upgrade the stores.

In 2006, the history of Famous-Barr came to an end. There would be no more store events, promotions, art exhibits and "Famous" people; now the story would be laid to rest in the archives department at the Missouri History Museum Library and Research Center. There are fifty-one boxes and several large scrapbooks holding half of the company's history in memos, press releases, photographs and newspaper articles. The rest of the company's ninety-five-year history is buried in city directories, newspaper archives, personal photograph collections and the former employees and customers whose lives intertwined with the daily business of Famous-Barr.

EPILOGUE

CLOSURE OF THE DOWNTOWN STORE IN ST. LOUIS

An era comes to an end.
—Sam Clark, retired Famous-Barr employee

Famous-Bar moved to the Railway Exchange Building in 1914, when the building opened in Downtown St. Louis, and wouldn't expand outside of the downtown area until 1948 when the store in Clayton was built.

After World War II, the downtown department stores were buzzing with activity; besides Famous-Barr at Sixth and Olive, there was Stix, Baer & Fuller at Seventh and Washington Avenue and Scruggs-Vandervoort-Barney at Olive and Ninth. Customers enjoyed fashion shows, dining and shopping downtown throughout the year, but at Christmas, the festivities at the downtown stores were what made the holiday season special. The stores competed with their winter wonderlands, enticing children to give Santa their Christmas lists and encouraging their parents to spend money. The store window displays brought crowds into the streets, where holiday music could be heard from outdoor speakers. The commotion with the traffic and the crowds in the streets was all part of getting into the Christmas spirit.

With business doing well and customers spending money downtown, Downtown Famous-Barr went through a renovation in 1955. The downtown allure lasted throughout most of the 1960s, but with the building of indoor shopping malls, customers started to desert downtown. They liked the convenience of free parking at the malls and not having to worry about the weather when going shopping from store to store. The first store to close downtown was Scruggs in 1967. Next, Stix, Baer & Fuller was purchased by Dillard's in 1984, and the Downtown Dillard's closed in 2001.

The central business district did try to breathe life back into the downtown retail industry. In 1985, St. Louis Centre Mall opened with four levels of shops, boutiques and restaurants. It was what the downtown business district hoped would be the resurgence of downtown. An article read, "May is proud to be a limited partner in this exciting project." The first four floors of the Famous-Barr flagship store, which connected to St. Louis Centre, went through a multimillion-dollar remodeling.

Downtown Famous-Barr kept holding on, making changes it hoped would improve business. When Macy's acquired Famous-Barr in 2006, it kept making changes to keep the downtown store open. In 2011, the store was remodeled and reduced to three sales floors. The intention was to serve downtown office workers and tourists. The merchandise selection was narrow, and the aisles were too quiet, even after the remodel. There just wasn't enough business to keep the doors open.

On May 20, 2013, the *St. Louis Post-Dispatch* published the article "Macy's to Close Downtown St. Louis Store." The end had come. St. Louis Macy's was not the only victim of struggling downtown businesses. In January 2013, Macy's had announced the closing of other downtown locations in St. Paul, Minnesota; Honolulu; and Houston.

The final clearance sale started on June 2, 2013, and lasted ten weeks. A number of the ninety-four store employees were offered positions in other St. Louis Macy's locations, while others were laid off. The one hundred Macy's corporate and district office employees from the ninth and tenth floor of the Railway Exchange Building were moved to Macy's Earth City location.

There had been a Famous-Barr in downtown St. Louis for ninety-five years when Macy's purchased Famous-Barr in 2006. The year 2014 would have marked the 100th anniversary of the Downtown Famous-Barr/Macy's store in the Railway Exchange Building, and it was a major disappointment that it didn't make it. So many people had walked through the doors and ridden the elevators and escalators of what was once the flagship store of Famous-Barr.

The closure of Downtown Macy's, the former Downtown Famous-Barr, brought about the end of an era. We are left with only our memories, as customers and employees whose lives were enhanced by Famous-Barr.

The business is gone, but the memories will remain in the stories we tell.

APPENDIX

FAMOUS-BARR RECIPES

Man can adjust to anything except not eating.
—Latin proverb

Manfred P. Zettl served as Famous-Barr's executive chef from 1964 to 1974. *Courtesy of Manfred P. Zettl.*

FAMOUS-BARR'S FRENCH ONION SOUP

3 pounds of peeled onions (5-pound bag of onions peeled will equal 3 pounds)
4 ounces butter or margarine
1½ teaspoons freshly ground pepper
2 tablespoons paprika
1 bay leaf
¼ cup flour (all purpose)
3 quarts canned beef bouillon
1 cup white wine (optional)
2 teaspoons salt

1. Slice onions ⅛" thick.
2. Melt butter, place onions in it, sauté slowly for 1½ hours in a large soup pot.
3. Add all other ingredients except bouillon, sauté over low heat 10 minutes more.
4. Add bouillon and simmer for 2 hours.
5. Adjust color to a rich brown with caramel coloring or kitchen bouquet.
6. Season with salt to taste.
7. Put in icebox overnight.

This recipe yields 2 quarts finished soup.

PROPER SERVING:
Heat soup. Fill fireproof casserole or individual fireproof bowls with 8 ounces of soup, top with three 1½" slices of Famous-Barr French bread and top with 1½ ounces imported Swiss or Gruyere cheese, place under broiler until brown, approximately five minutes at 550 degrees.

FAMOUS-BARR CHEESECAKE

In 1953, the Famous-Barr Cheesecake was on the menu and cost fifteen cents a slice.

CRUST:
1 cup graham cracker crumbs
1 tablespoon sugar
½ teaspoon cinnamon
1 tablespoon butter, melted

FILLING:

5 (8 ounces each) packages cream cheese
1¾ cups sugar
3 Tbsp flour
1½ teaspoons grated orange rind
5 eggs
2 egg yolks
¼ cup milk

Preheat oven to 475 degrees. Lightly grease a 9-inch Springform pan.

Combine first 3 ingredients and blend in melted butter. Press firmly over bottom of pan. Chill briefly before filling.

Let cheese soften in large bowl; blend in sugar, flour and rind. Beat with electric mixer until light and fluffy. Add eggs and yolks, one at a time, beating well after each addition. Stir in milk and pour into crumb crust.

Bake at 475 degrees 10 minutes. Reduce oven temperature to 200 degrees and bake 1 hour. Let cool in oven another hour; remove and cool on wire rack.

ECLAIRS

Recipe from Chef Honsack at Famous-Barr Clayton store

13 ounces flour
10 ounces butter
2 ounces sugar
¼ quart water
12 eggs
Pinch salt

Melt butter. Add salt, sugar and water. Add flour. Cook on low heat until dough follows spoon around pan. Take off heat, add eggs one at a time. Put through pastry bag on lightly greased cooked sheet in éclair shapes. Bake at 350 degrees for 12–15 minutes or until golden. Split when cool and fill with ice cream, or chocolate or strawberry mousse. Top with icing if desired.

DUTCH APPLE BEIGNETS

From the Petits Chefs cooking school for kids, taught by Famous-Barr executive chef Jan G. Verdonkschot

4 large apples
Juice of 2 lemons
2½ cups all-purpose flour, sifted
¼ teaspoon salt
1½ tablespoon granulated sugar
4 eggs
1½ cups light cream
2 pounds solid vegetable shortening
1 cup granulated sugar
2 tablespoons ground cinnamon
1 cup all-purpose flour

Core apples, peel and slice into ¼-inch-thick pieces. Place apple slices in lemon juice immediately so they won't turn brown. Combine the sifted flour, salt, and 1½ tablespoons sugar; mix well. Beat eggs and cream together; add gradually to flour mixture. Stir well. Let batter rest 10 minutes.

Melt shortening in a pot suitable for deep-frying. Combine 1 cup sugar and cinnamon for cinnamon-sugar; set aside.

Roll apple slices in the remaining cup of flour; dip in batter, letting excess batter drip off. Fry in hot fat until both sides of the apple are well browned. Drain cooked beignets on paper towels, and then roll in cinnamon-sugar mixture. Serve hot.

Yield: 8 servings.

JOHN WHITE BURGER

Famous-Barr, the Jade Room Restaurant

RAREBIT SAUCE FOR JOHN WHITE BURGER
½ pound American cheese, cut into thin slices
¾ cup half-and-half
1 teaspoon Worcestershire sauce
½ teaspoon dry mustard

Place cheese in the top of a double boiler. Add half-and-half, Worcestershire sauce and mustard. Cook over medium heat, stirring occasionally, until cheese melts. Slice onions thinly, and then cook them in ½ inch of hot oil or shortening. Remove onions when they are light brown and crispy; if you cook them too long, they will become bitter. Drain well on paper towels.

To assemble the burgers, use toasted buns, grilled or broiled hamburger patties made from ground beef that is 85 percent lean, the onions and a rarebit sauce thick enough to stay on the burgers.
Yield: 4 servings.

***

The following recipes were printed in the Bridal Registry and given out to attendees at the "Bride of the '90s" event at the Northwest Famous-Barr store on February 17, 1990.

Raspberry Honey Walnut Salad

1 head romaine lettuce
1 cup red raspberries or strawberries (frozen, if no fresh are available)
1 cup blackberries or blueberries or canned mandarin orange segments
1 cup walnuts

Clean and dry lettuce. Tear into small pieces. Toss lettuce and fruit with raspberry honey dressing until well blended. Top with walnuts. Serve and enjoy!

Raspberry Honey Dressing

¼ cup raspberry vinegar
4 tablespoons walnut oil
3 tablespoons honey

In a small bowl, combine all ingredients and whisk until well blended.

Chicken Breast with Juniper Berries under Blueberry Sauce

4 chicken breasts, boned with skin removed
3 tablespoons olive oil
16 juniper berries
Fresh milled black pepper to taste

Dry meat to ensure proper browning; season meat with fresh milled pepper to taste. In heated skillet, add olive oil and juniper berries. Add chicken breasts to skillet; turn to brown on both sides. When juices run clear (approximately 15 minutes), meat is done. Remove breasts from skillet and arrange on platter. Top with blueberry sauce and serve.

Blueberry Sauce

1 pint blueberries
2 tablespoons sugar
3 thin slices lemon
1 tablespoon lemon juice

Place all ingredients in a small saucepan over medium heat. Heat until sugar melts, stirring frequently. Pour over prepared meat.

Hinode Wild Rice with Curry

1 cup Hinode Wild Rice Mix
3 cups chicken broth
1 tablespoon dehydrated onions
1 tablespoon curry powder
2 tablespoons fresh minced parsley
3 tablespoons butter

Place all ingredients in a electric rice cooker and turn on. If you do not have an electric rice cooker, prepare the rice as you usually do on your stove or in the microwave.

CHOCOLATE PLUNGE

⅔ cup Karo Dark Syrup
½ cup whipping cream
2 packages (4 oz. each) Baker's Sweet German Chocolate,
or
1 package (8 oz.) Baker's Semi-Sweet Chocolate

Coarsely chop chocolate. Stir syrup and cream together in a medium saucepan. Bring to a boil over medium heat and stir in chopped chocolate. Stir until completely melted. Serve warm as a dip with fresh fruit.

MISSISSIPPI MUD CAKE

This recipe is from Betty Manning (one of Famous-Barr's security checkers), printed in the Famous-Barr Northwest Plaza 1975 newsletter Plaza Press, Jaco's Cooking Corner. Jaco's Cooking Corner *was created by Jean Jaco in* Town and Country. *People would send her recipes. She would try them, and if she liked them, she would send them to the managers of the* Plaza Press.

2 cups sugar
1 cup oil
4 eggs
1½ cup of flour
1 jar marshmallow crème
⅓ cup cocoa
3 teaspoons vanilla
1 cup chopped pecans
¼ teaspoon salt

Cream sugar, oil; add eggs and beat by hand. Sift flour, cocoa, and salt. Add to above mixture. Mix, add vanilla and nuts. Bake at 350 degrees for 30 minutes in a long loaf pan (13½" x 9" x 2"). Remove from oven and cool 10 minutes. Spread marshmallow crème over top.

CAKE ICING

1 stick unsalted butter
3 tablespoons cocoa
1 box powdered sugar
½ cup canned milk
1 teaspoon vanilla
1 cup chopped pecans

Sift sugar and cocoa; mix with melted butter. Add canned milk and vanilla, stir in nuts and spread over marshmallow crème. Let icing set.

STRAWBERRY DAIQUIRI

This recipe from Mrs. Billings in the Lingerie Department was also printed in Jaco's Cooking Corner.

1 can frozen lemonade
1 can rum
1 package frozen strawberries

Mix in blender. Add about 8 or 10 ice cubes, mix in blender again. Serve.

GERMAN APPLE CAKE

This recipe from Mary Hancock was printed in the July 1976 Famous-Barr Downtown newsletter Famous-Barr This & That.

5 apples
5 tablespoons sugar
2 teaspoons cinnamon
3 cups un-sifted flour
2⅓ cups sugar
½ teaspoon salt
4 eggs, unbeaten

1 cup cooking oil
2 teaspoons vanilla
⅓ cup orange juice
1½ teaspoons baking soda
1½ teaspoons baking powder

Pare apples and cut into thin slices. Mix sugar and cinnamon, sprinkle over apples and toss. Set aside. Place in mixing bowl, flour, sugar, salt, eggs, oil, vanilla, and orange juice. Blend together with mixer on low speed for one minute, then three minutes at medium speed. Add baking soda and baking powder. Mix one minute longer. Grease tube pan and fill with alternating layers of batter and sliced apples (three layers of batter and two of apples, beginning and ending with batter). Bake at 350 degrees for 1½ hours. Serves 10–12.

TORTE

This recipe was printed in the February 1977 Famous-Barr newsletter South County Grapevine.

Mix 1 stick butter, 1 cup flour, 2 tablespoons sugar, and ¾ cup chopped pecans. Pat dough in 9" x 13" pan. Bake 15 minutes or until brown at 350 degrees. Cool. Mix 8 ounces cream cheese with 1 cup powdered sugar. Fold in ½ of a 9½ ounce container of Pet Whip. Spread over crust. Cook 2 packages of coconut cream pudding with 3 cups milk. When cool spread over other layers. Top with remaining ½ package of Pet Whip. Refrigerate several hours or overnight.

BIBLIOGRAPHY

Books

Corbett, Katherine T. *In Her Place*. St. Louis: Missouri Historical Society Press, 1999.

Dry, Camille N. *Pictorial Saint Louis, The Great Metropolis of the Mississippi Valley.* Edited by Rich J. Compton. St. Louis, MO: Compton & Company, 1875.

Gray, Rockwell. *A Century of Enterprise: St. Louis, 1894–1994*. St. Louis: Missouri Historical Society Press, 1994.

Pennington, Gail. "Fans at Galleria Are Live with Kathie Lee," *St. Louis Post-Dispatch*, March 26, 1992.

Pepín, Jacques. *The Apprentice: My Life in the Kitchen*. New York: Houghton Mifflin Company, 2003.

Rademacher, Diane. *Famous Firsts of St. Louis.* St. Louis, MO: Diane Rademacher, in conjunction with Mound City Publishing, 2014.

Stadler, Frances Hurd. *St. Louis Day by Day.* St. Louis, MO: Patrice Press, 1989.

Straus, J.C. *Planter's Hotel: Fourth Street, Chestnut to Pine, St. Louis, Missouri*. St. Louis, MO: I. Haas & Company, 1895.

Taylor, Jacob N., and M.O. Crooks. *Sketch Book of St. Louis.* St. Louis, MO: George Knapp & Company, Printers and Binders, 1858.

RESOURCES FROM THE MISSOURI HISTORY MUSEUM LIBRARY AND RESEARCH CENTER IN ST. LOUIS

Archives: Famous-Barr Publicity Department Records, 2008.
The Bulletin/Missouri Historical Society. Volume XVI, 1959–60.
The Bulletin/Missouri Historical Society. Volume XXIII, 1966–67.
The Bulletin/Missouri Historical Society. Volume XXX, 1973–74.
Central Magazine, March 1874.
Mercantile and Manufacturing Scrapbooks, Volumes 3, 6.
Missouri Historical Society, Historic Homes of Missouri. Volume VI.
Missouri Historical Society, Old Public Buildings of St. Louis. Volume I.
Necrologies & Other Materials. Volume 2P.
Newsletters: Landmarks Letter, Volume 16, November 1981.
Reedy, W.M. *St. Louis To-Day, Special Issue of the Mirror*, May 9, 1912.
Scrapbook: Sarah B. Hull, 1891–96.
Scrapbook: Walter B. Stevens, Volume 84
St. Louis City Directories, 1849–1911.
Vertical File/Famous-Barr

WEBSITES

Annalee Artist Dolls. http://www.suecoffee.com/About-Annalee-Thorndike.html
Bird in Hand Shop. http://www.stlmag.com/A-Conversation-with-Evelyn-Newman/
Bombeck, Erma. http://www.imdb.com
Children's Miracle Network. http://www.cmn-stl.org
Dannebaum, Julia. http://articles.philly.com/2011-12-28/news/30565505_1_susanna-foo-french-cooking-creative-cooking-school
Fair St. Louis. http://www.fairsaintlouis.org
Famous-Barr. http://community.tasteofhome.com/community_forums/f/30/p/191788/2593444.aspx#2593444
Famous-Barr. http://departmentstoremuseum.blogspot.com/search?q=Famous-Barr
Famous-Barr Cheesecake. http://www.bakespace.com/recipes/detail/Famous-Barr%20Cheesecake/40311/#.VCCO7E0tDIU
Gibson, Bob. http://www.baseball-reference.com

Guempel, David. http://www.stljewishlight.com/special_sections/dining_guide/
Jahan, Marine. http://www.imdb.com
John White Burgers. http://pattietierney.blogspot.com/2011/04/famous-barrs-john-white-burger.html
Kersee, Jackie-Joyner. http://www.usatf.org/HallOfFame
Macy's. http://www.stltoday.com/business/local/macy-s-announcement-a-belated-nod-to-the-fall-of/article_cde24361-033e-528d-9a6b-7d01d77561ce.html
May, David. http://www.immigrantentrepreneurship.org
Monroe, Vaughn. http://www.vaughnmonroesociety.org
Musial, Stan. http://www.baseball-reference.com
Newman, Evelyn. http://www.stlmag.com/home/The-Collector-039s-Cache-House/
ProQuest Historical Newspapers: St. Louis Post-Dispatch (1874–1922). http://mohistory.org/node/7208
Schoendienst, Red. http://www.baseball-reference.com
Smith, Ozzie. http://www.baseball-reference.com
St. Louis Senior Olympics. http://www.stlouisseniorolympics.org
Tyson, Cicely. http://www.imdb.com
Veiled Prophet. http://www.veiledprophet.org
Verdonkschot, Jan. http://acfchefsdecuisinestlouis.org/about.php
Weiss, Helen. http://www.bizjournals.com/stlouis/search?q=%22Helen+Weiss%22&title=%20title=
Zettl, Manfred P. http://acfchefsdecuisinestlouis.org/about.php
Zettl, Manfred P. http://www.westendword.com/articles-c-2012-04-11-179903.114137-soups-on.html#axzz3E53st11v

INDEX